STRICTLY WESTERN
COWBOY POETRY

The west is dead my Friend
  But writers hold the seed
  And what they saw
  will live and grow
Again to those who read

C. M. Russell
1917

I prefer the wide open spaces where lawyers never go. But even in the cowboy poetry book world, some legal words need said; this I know.

STRICTLY WESTERN COWBOY POETRY

First Edition

Copyright © 1998 by Donald C. Decker

Library of congress cataloging in Publication Data

ISBN # 0-9649790-3-9

Visit Basic Western Book Company on the Web at:

www.basicwesternbook.com

Acknowledgements

This cowboy word painter wishes to acknowledge all the people who have helped make this Western Poetry book the great enjoyment it has been.

To all the folks who have been part of my cowboy and horseman life, I dedicate this book. There have been many. Some remember the great adventures, others may not. I remember them all and thank them.

It has been a most interesting trail. Sometimes with a lot of sunshine, sometimes kind of tough; still it has been great. In all my travels the western trail has been best for me.

My special thanks to my wife and publisher, Basic Western Book Company, for her encouragement and belief in me. Gloria Grace Fisher Decker has empowered my poetry and my life.

Barry Holt has spent hours at the computer with me in technical work and book design. Thank you so much! The cover, which is our logo, was done by Jana Sol.

Hope you all enjoy the book as much as we have had putting it together! **D.C. Decker**

Howdy Folks,

Ol' friends n' new pardners, come along and ride with me. I'll tell ya' some western tales n' some rhymin' ones you see. I've put em' down in words to tell so you can understand em' quite well. Put your self deep in the west n' read of the tales I love best. Ride along n' live these western ways 'cause it was mighty excitin' in those good old days. The west is still romantic, friend n' it's ok ta' dream; for way out here is a big ol' stage n' it's a mighty grand scene. Come get in the saddle n' you will soon see, the west has lots of space n' good folks n' it's sure a nice place ta' be.

D.C. Decker... Humble Word Slinger

CONTENTS

Cowboy Stories & Dreams 39

Cowboy Lovin' 57

Live The Legend!

'BOUT COWBOY POETRY

THE FIRST PART OF THIS COWBOY'S POETRY BOOK LETS ME TELL SOME OF MY THOUGHTS ABOUT COWBOY POETRY ITSELF. I'VE BEEN A TRAININ' HORSES AND WORKIN' CATTLE MOST OF MY LIFE, WITH OTHER EXCITIN' THINGS THROWN IN. I HAVE ALWAYS WANTED TO BE A WORD PAINTER. HOPE YOU LIKE MY STRICTLY WESTERN POETRY. I NEARLY AGREE WITH OUR OLD FRIEND OF THE WEST CHARLIE RUSSELL.

I STILL THINK THAT ARTISTS HOLD THE SEED OF THE OLD WEST BETTER THAN WORD PAINTERS, BUT OF COURSE I AIN'T NO ARTIST.   DCD.

betwine the pen and the brush there is little difference but I believe the man that makes word pictures is the greater

-C. M. Russell

1

RIDE A CARING TRAIL

To all the fine cowboys n' cowgirls.
The young n' old who dare.
We who care,
sometimes in pain we bear.
We who are aware,
our hearts in pain,
and still we care..

D.C.Decker.... Caring word Painter

PARDNER,
EVEN IF THEY BUCK, RIDE EM' SMOOTH.....
                          D.C.

OLD POETS PEN

What is a poem anyway, of what value to mankind?
Perhaps a healing for the soul or a vision for the blind.
The capture of an instant, a remembered beauty rare.
An unshed tear of yesteryear, a quiet unspoken prayer.

An utterance of emotion from sheltered depths of soul.
A laughing troutstream's murmuring, amber waves that roll.
A fine horse loping while some cowboy sings a song.
The caress of ones beloved, the hero's arm so strong.

There is no act or story a poet cannot reveal.
No emotion, pain or happiness the poet cannot feel.
For all of life and living can be illuminated when,
Wisdom, truth and beauty are awakened by a poets pen......

D.C. Decker...........Romantic Cowboy Word Painter

COWBOY POETRY
GATHERIN'

We're all here to tell our tales
in that earthy western sound.
Here we meet to spend some time
so all you cowboy n' cowgirl poets gather round.
To talk n' learn of many things
n' tell em' all in words that rhyme.

Cause poetry can expose this heart of mine!

It talks of many things,
of love n' cowboys n' kings.
Sure enough it is an art,
the skill of words ya' see.
Some that rhyme n' some that don't,
Still, we call it poetry.

D.C. Decker....   *Cowboy Word Painter*

I recon you all understand my simple poem. But let me give it to you another way. The
meaning of POETRY by my old friend and colleague Mr. D. Webster:

*The production of a poet. Writing that formulates a concentrated, imaginative awareness
of experience in language chosen and arranged to create a specific emotional response
through meaning, sound and rhythm. A quality that stirs the imagination; a quality of
spontaneity and grace..............Dan Webster*

THAT'S THE WAY WEBSTER TELLS IT.

I Say it Like this.
Sure sounds fine as wine to this ol' hand.
I'll give it my all to do the best I can.
I hope I don't get confused by this fancy meanin'.
I was thinkin' poetry was more like a cleanin'.
Tellin' what the heart n' soul was wantin'
to tell out of this dusty ol' mind;
to tell the stories about folks of my kind.
I'll just say it my way in the sweet by n' by.
Even if it might cause a sensitive one ta' cry.

Ol' D.C.   *Humble Cowboy Word Slinger*

I WRITE COWBOY POETRY

We were standin' by this old corral
a talkin' 'bout the west.
This feller says, "I recon ya' can't ride worth a damn,
what is it that you do best?

"I write cowboy poetry,"
I told em' straight n' true.
"No man, what do ya' do fer a livin',
tell me somethin' useful that you do."

"Pardner, I write great words on paper
or on the bunkhouse walls,
or in the horsebarn
I write em' on the stalls."

"Well ain't ya' somethin',"
the ol' boy says right soon.
"I'll bet ya' write on the spur of the moment
settin' in the ol' tack room."

"I recon you'd squat with your spurs on
to set n' write a line."
The ol' boy was a laughin' at me,
n' I was a bidin' my time.

"Big boy let me tell ya',
writin' words comes from the heart.
Bein' a word painter ain't no easy life,
but for me it's just a part."

"Sure I love ta' put words ta' feelin's
no matter what I do .
But, let me tell ya' stranger,
I'll damn sure out ride you!

D.C. Decker.....Cowboy Word Painter....

COWBOY STORY TELLER

I recon I've told many a yarn,
n' some were true ya' know.
Used ta' go out ta' the old barn
n' think em' up n' go.

Most of em' were real life things
made bigger by my mind.
When I think of em' the old bell rings.
Some were rank n' wild n' some were very kind.

I still love ta' tell the stories,
simple words are mighty things.
They tell of hardships n' glories,
they fly about as on Eagles wings.

One time in Oklahoma it was too windy
to set up our round-up tent.
I asked an old man, "Pop, does it blow this way all the time?"
"No son, it blows the other way part of the time."

A whole lot of cowhands were story tellers too.
There were not bald face liars like so many say,
they were just romantics when they talked to you.
The "Big Windys" had their place, this is very true.

Cowboys love horses, women, hot biscuits,
n' beefsteak.
With their wild ol' yarns
they'd sure could take the cake.

Besides bein' a story teller
I've trained lots of animals too.
I trained a good huntin' hound fer a feller,
his name was just Ol' blue.

When I returned his dawg he asked me how it went.
I told em' he was a very good dawg n' had a good scent.
But ever so often he stops, holds one foot up
n' his tail gets stiff as a board; but I broke em' of that.

Well, I'll always be a cowboy story teller
n' tell a few big lies 'cause it's fun fer you.
I'll bring in lots of color fer ya' feller,
fer a cowboys life has got ta' be entertainin' too!

D.C. Decker......... Sorry Cowboy Story Teller

OL' COWBOY'S WORDS

In all my travels n' work in the west
I've always tried to do my best.
But when I sit to tell or recite
I sometimes hurt a mite.

My inspiration for words of life
comes on occasion from the depths of strife.
Not so much from mind or tongue,
but from my breath n' soul undone.

I recon the pain of life is worth the trip
even when my emotion needs put to script.
Without written word or a stories mood
no one but God knew where I stood.

My love n' yearnin's would never be known
no one on earth would know I'd grown.
Without the power of words to tell
the inmost secrets of my life to dwell.

For in the quiet of my mind
I expose the wonderment of humankind.
Can allow the deepest thoughts to dwell
and put them down in words that tell.

I'm probably not too good at poetry
not very smooth with rhymes.
but I try to get my feelin's across
n' I often do at times.

Can't say my life's been simple,
didn't make it easy as can be.
But I'll do my best to tell ya',
usin' my own kind of poetry!

D.C. Decker....   Word Painter
                       Cowboy Poet
                       Philosopher

10

COWBOYS, WORD TALKIN'

DREAMIN' OF ELKO

I want to go up there to Elko
so I can get up on their stage.
I want to go up there to Elko
so I can tell em' bout ridin' the range.

Heard they have fine cowboy poets there,
who can tell it like it was.
The old timers n' the young un's
I recon the place is abuzz.

I sure want to go up to Elko
so I can recite a poem or two.
I'll tell em' how I rode em'
in the days of '22.

I damned sure want to go up to Elko
so I can tell em' of my cowboy ways.
I'll tell em' of the roundups
n' how we spent our days.

If they would let me go up to Elko
n' get up on their stage,
I just might tell em' bout our night life,
cause it was a hell of a rage!

I sure hope I get up there to Elko
so I can tell em' of those western days.
When all the livestock was rank n' wild
n' how I rode em' in my cowboy ways!

D.C. Decker...................Cowboy Poet N' Word Painter

WESTERN COW FOLKS LIFE

THESE ARE POEMS ABOUT
COWBOY AND RANCH LIFE. SOME
OF THEM ARE ABOUT THINGS
I'VE DONE N' SOME ARE MERELY
DREAMS. SOME ARE ABOUT
RANCH FOLKS I'VE KNOWN N'
THINGS THEY HAVE DONE.
LIKE WILL ROGERS, I'VE NEVER
MET COW FOLKS I DIDN'T LIKE.
WELL, I'D SURE LIKE TA' BE LIKE
HIM.

14

WILL JAMES

I've felt the spirit of Will James
most all of my life.
We have a lot in common
including some major strife.

But that is just a part of life,
a part all have to endure.
The rest was dreams fulfilled;
some great ones you can be sure.

Both born on the east side of the tracks
n' yearnin' to be out west.
We wanted to be a cowboyin'
n' we was fixin' ta' be the best.

Will made it to western Canada
at a very early age.
But he was hankerin' for Montana
in the tall grass n' the sage.

He worked for many an outfit
including the CS brand.
Down in New Mexico
he made a real good hand.

He'd draw on bunkhouse walls,
n' the folks round liked his art.
He'd draw on anything
n' in his life his art became a part.

He was a good horseman
but one day he had a bad fall.
Happy bucked em' off on the RR tracks
n' a doctor they did call.

At twenty eight Happy convinced him
to ride the rough ones no more.
It was his Turning Point
towards words n' art to score.

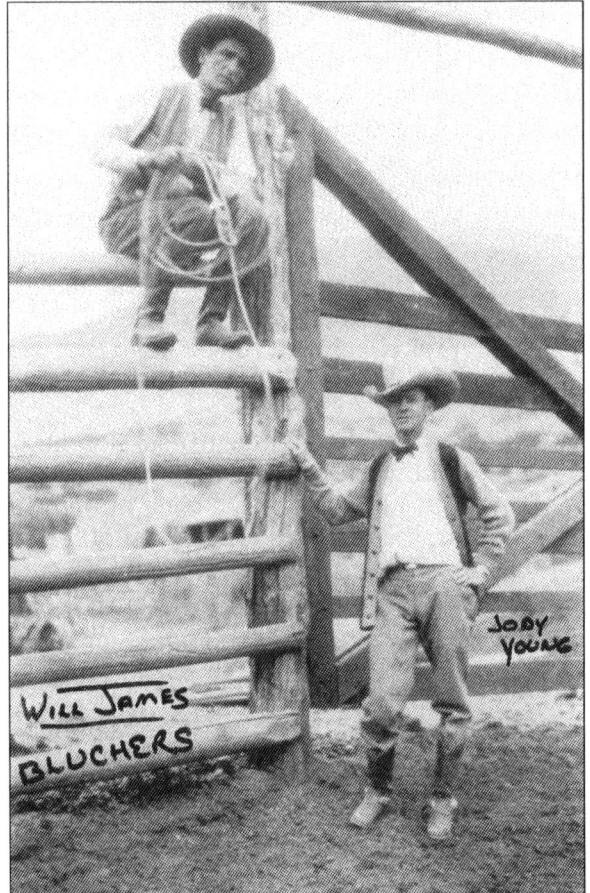

15

He was a natural genius,
one of the finest in the land.
He was a cowboy like Charlie Russell
n' he made an all around hand.

Yes, he was a Drifting Cowboy
Nevada n' Montana he called home.
He settled down on the Rockin' R
expectin' to never more roam.

In 1926 he wrote Smoky The Cowhorse
n' won the Newberry prize.
Wrote and illustrated about 28 books,
a great feat in anyone's eyes.

His life was full of accomplishment
it went from shore to shore.
From New York to Los Angeles
who could ask for anything more.

He met the famous n' common man
and treated them all just fine.
But I believe he was most at home
on the ranch n' range most of the time.

But friends I'm here ta' tell ya'
as a true westerner he was the best.
In his spiritual quest to be out west
he surely passed the test.

You all know this could go on and on
his story is filled with romance on call.
No, he wasn't perfect
but he damned sure impressed us all.

At six years old I got hold
of Young Cowboy don't ya' see.
My life was never the same n'
it made a pretty good cowboy out of me.

Folks, it sure makes one proud
ta' see ya' gathered here.
To honor such a man
that our God created so dear.   D.C. Decker   <u>Lover of the spirit of Will James</u>

16

THE DRIFTING COWBOY

When the works all done this fall,
Before the winter days begin.
I'm goin' ta' ride toward the sunset
n' have a great time that just won't end.

For all the cows I've herded in the west,
God knows I'm due a rest.
No more cows around ta' punch,
It's fall, we finished our last bunch.

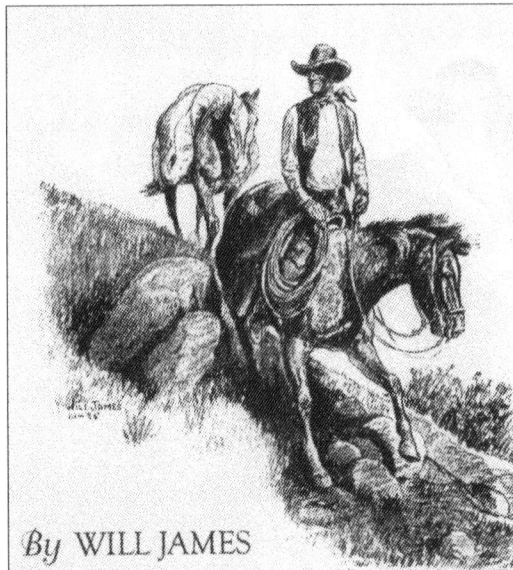

By WILL JAMES

I'll saddle ol' Stranger, he's black n' fast.
A solid hoss ya' know can last.
I'll lead ol' Blue, he's good n' true,
He's tough n' strong n' he'll foller you.

I'll load the Decker pack n' hitch.
Ya' can trust ol' Blue he'd never pitch.
It's sunrise now, we're headin' west,
Out the ol' ranch gate full of zest!

It's a beautiful morn; the wind blows a gust.
The horses don't mind they're used ta' the dust.
I dallies ol' Blue ta' my saddle horn.
I'm just so happy it's a beautiful morn.

I've heard in the past, it's time ta' ride fast.
I feel a northern a driftin' this way.
Can be hard on a hand n' his horses too.
At least that's what the old timers say.

I'm a ridin' along just ta' singin' a song.
Got my hosses n' gear, I can't go wrong.
The prairie looks great under a sky of blue.
A cowboys life is good n' true.

I puts my spurs against Strangers side.
Ol' Blue just follers, bless his hide.
We're lopin' down this grassy plain.
All of a sudden comes a cold rain.

I pressed my spurs harder, I rode in a breeze.
Looks down a draw where there were some trees.
Just right for a campsite, I'll give it a try.
Sure enough was perfect with a creek runnin' by.

Hobbled the horses so they could graze.
Rain had now stopped, just left a haze.
Laid out the camp, unrolled my sack.
Built me a fire, unpacked the pack.

After grub, it was the best,
I watched the sunset in the west.
Darkness came in awhile,
Watched the fire glow with a smile.

Up by a tree on a knoll,
I spread out my ol' bedroll.
As I lay down ta' sleep,
I thanked God for my keep.

In the silence of the night I heard the coyotes howl.
Heard a screechin' sound, was just a wise old owl.
Then I heard this stompin' so I'm lookin' out my bag.
I might have known it was the horses a playin' tag.

Finally sleep had come, I was at peace that night.
My dreams were clear, I saw with keen insight,
Foundations I had laid, the long, long trail I'd made
With wisdom clear n' the love of God so dear.

When the mornin' sunrise began ta' hit my eyes
I jumped from my bedroll n' ta' my surprise,
There stood Stranger n' ol' Blue, they're tried n' true.
Like a good ol' sidekick, they'd never leave you.

They'd been grazin' all night n' drinkin' from the creek.
It was time for chuck my hunger was dire, so I fixed the fire.
Coffees great n' the pancakes too, ate quite a few.
Broke the camp, saddled up n' put the pack back on ol' Blue.

With hobbles off I mounted up n' rode over the crest.
I was the happiest cowboy again a headin' west.
Ridin' Stranger n' leadin' ol' Blue had ta' be the best.
Compadres in our Vision Quest, I knew we'd pass the test.

Our long n' windin' trail, over mountains n' vale,
from sunrise ta' sunset, through sunshine n' hail.
By God's Holy Grace, we'll manage the problems we face.
I'll ride my circles wide, til I'm called ta' the great divide!

D.C. Decker

**I dedicate this poem to my brother Tom W. Decker on his birthday.
It is April 19, 1998. I give this poem to a man of many talents! I give
this poem to a true All-Around Champion. He could ride a great buckin'
horse and take good are of his wonderful family. We have been blessed
with God's Grace. He holds it high. Praise God for my precious brother.**

THE COWBOY N' THE CRITTER

'Twas an overcast day with skies of gray
in the woods it was quiet n' still,
except for the rustlin' leaves of the scrub oak trees
that shivered in the wind as they fell.

The woods were scattered over rugged terrain,
cut through by a rocked ribbed ravine,
which ran headlong into Dry Gulch Pass
bordered by bluffs that overlooked a stream.

A lone cowboy, nearly a legend in his time,
atop Round Mountain Ridge he rode,
with sturdy rein n' saddle tight
like a ghost from the past in days of old.

A leather chapped man in denim,
fair haired n' sun weathered skin,
the lines of his character made visible
as he winced in the blowing wind.

Will Everidge

The silence of the woods was broken,
by the bellerin' of a Hereford calf,
that wandered astray n' been lost for days,
ramblin' around in Dry Gulch Pass.

The cowboy raised up his reins,
heard the bellerin' n' spotted the calf,
as his horse picked his way
down the slopes of ol' Dry Gulch Pass.

The cowboy approached the hairy little critter,
the whiteface calf with no defense,
sayin', "Come on little doggie, I'm takin' you home,
n' from now on I'll make sure you stay fenced.

The calf's energy was exhausted,
he wasn't up ta' givin' much of a struggle,
the cowboy, with concern, gently lifted the calf
so as to push em' up over his saddle.

The sure footed horse plodded cautiously
up the slopes of the rocky ravine,
each slip of the hoof sending rocks below
sounded like crashes n' screams.

Soon the cowboy breathed a sigh of relief,
the horse flared his nostrils n' snorted,
the little whiteface calf gave it his best
n' with a swish of his tail he retorted.

It was all in a day's ridin' approachin' Round Mountain
n' findin' their way back home,
when the rusty old gate threw open it's arms,
the ol' cowboy knew this calf would never more roam.

In seasons to come this lone cowboy
will ever ride the ridge atop those hills,
he'll take care of the stock, a vanishin' breed
this cowboy known as "Will."

I WANT TA' BE A COWBOY

I want to be a cowboy,
and with the cowboys stand.
With leather chaps n' boots n' hats
and a lariat in my hand.

Right now I'm just a greenhorn
waitin' ta' learn the trade.
I want ta' be tough n' macho;
tough as rawhide n' tailor made.

I want ta' be a bronc buster
n' ride a buckin' horse.
I'll scratch em' in the shoulders,
with my silver spurs of course.

I'll rake em' up and down his side;
you bet I'll fan the breeze.
I'll ride my silver saddle
n' ride em' with great ease.

I want ta' be a cowboy
n' work in the big outside.
So I can ride in a cowherd,
n' cut one high n' wide.

On Friday night I'll get ta' town,
a cowboy? I'll make it slick!
At punchin' cows I know I'll shine.
<u>But brother, I can't dance a lick.</u>

D. C. Decker......Cowboy Word Painter

22

LONELY COYOTES HOWL

As I ride my ol' hoss
o'r the great prairies
n' night time falls around us
in the setting of the sun.
After the cattles been tended
n' the long days work is done,
I hear this strange eery callin'
right after the cattle quit bawlin'....

It's a lonely howl a comin'
across the windy hills.
It's sings of blood upon the trail
n' bellies to be filled.
Tis as haunting as the laughter
of loves first awkward try.
As old as the song the wild goose sings
of adventures in the sky....................

It's dark as deepest midnight.
It holds courage to meet life.
It's primitive n' savage
as killin' with a knife.
It sets the air to throbbing.
It makes one want to sway
in the darkness that tells the tale
n' finds it's lonely way......................

It tells of things that have no words,
of things man can't endure.
When he must seek the walls of home
n' pray for something pure!
It sings of night n' cold n' pain,
of death beneath it's cowl.
It seems to hold the sorrows of the world,
THAT LONESOME COYOTES HOWL!

D.C. Decker......   Lonesome Cowboy Word Painter.....

23

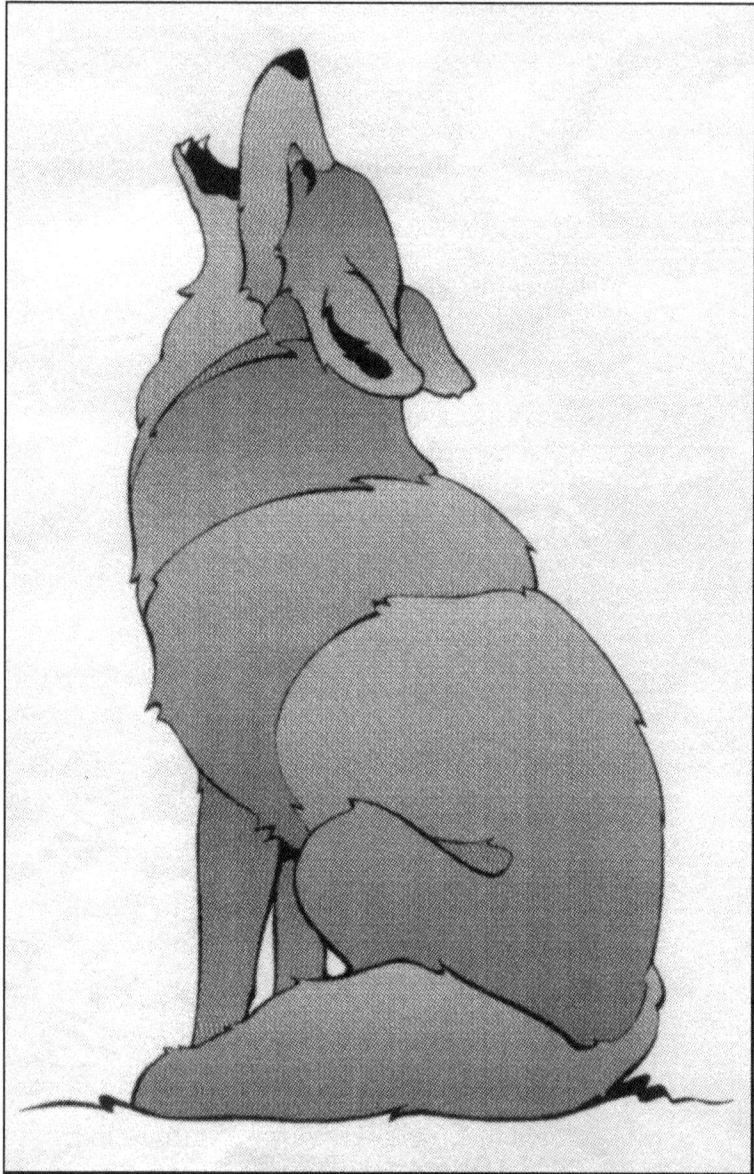

BREAKIN' WILD ONES

Was breakin' wild ones ta' get along.
Got most all of em' rode.
Some were big n' strong
n' on some I plumb got throwed.

We'd run in this herd
a tryin' ta' impress ol' Erd.
He was the rancher
who owned this whole herd.

Came on this little mare, stood 14-2.
She'd never packed a saddle
n' she never wore a shoe.
To say she was rank I'll leave it to you.

The mare was pretty n' she was fast
I'll try ta' ride her like in the past.
I've been a good bronc buster
so I'll give her a go but I might not last.

I wanted a job on this Cross Bell Ranch
n' the boss was seeing how I'd stand.
If I took ta' settin' on the mare
I'd better not hit the sand.

The boss looked me over
n' he said in advance,
"Yes if you can ride her
I'll give ya' a chance."

A pickin' up my saddle
I went on through the gate.
When a cowhand says ta' me,
"Shake hands before it's too late."

When I went ta' rope her
my rope went into a stall.
I built a loop n' threw it
n' the dang thing caught nothin' at all.

I gathered up my rope once more,
believe me I was a getting' sore.
The boss was a watchin' every move
n' was grouchy ta' the core.

Then I pulled another throw
n' just by chance ya' see,
the rope landed hard n' fast
a little above her knee.

I jerked her ta' the snubbin' post
n' took up all the slack.
Picked up my hackamore n' rein,
slipped it on her n' rubbed her back.

The look she gave this young cowboy
could nearly kill em' dead.
She rolled her eyes toward the sky
n' started a throwin' her head.

Picked up my ol' saddle
n' placed it on her back.
"Stand," I says, "ya critter",
'till I pull down this cache.

I'll turn ya' loose when I get set
n' get my rein in hand.
I'll ride ya' sure n' ya' can bet
the boss will know I can.

I climbed into the saddle
on that Cross Bell 7-T.
I shouted, "Powder River,
turn her loose to me!"

Ol' Flint undone the dallies,
stepped back to watch the fun.
The way she went to pitchin',
a pitchin' on the run.

I quick got down to ridin',
a ridin' her for fair.
The way I was a scratchin'
y'd know that I was there.

I hit her in the shoulder.
Then is when I sighed,
the ol' mare gave her best
n' I knew that I could ride.

She bucked so hard
my face was red.
She was a great bucker,
the best would dread.

When the dust had settled
and she was lead away,
The boss came up
and said that I could stay.

"You're sure hired now son,
we know you can ride a tough one.
This string is in your hands
but your day has just begun."

The boss looked me in the eye,
"You're quite a hand D.C.
You can go to the big Rodeo
and win a prize for me!"

D.C. Decker

RANCHIN' BY CHOICE

When you look at all the choices
in this life that we make.
A ranchers life is a divine one:
even in the setting of the sun.

In all the world it must be rare
to find a life that can compare.
A cowhands life is next to the earth,
n' he loves it all for all he's worth.

If you'll look across the oceans of grass,
flowers on the prairies, a mighty mass.
You'd know right then the Creators there,
for they bring beauty in sunlights glare.

As a true cowhand rides the rounds
n' gathers in the cattle's bounds:
he just can't help but see
the natural beauty of Divinity.

If you choose to ride under the western sky,
n' bein' close to mother nature is your cry.
I recon you've made the right choice at least.
'Cause there your soul will find perfect peace.

Folks, we know it is a special life
this ranchin' and it's strife.
It's still great punchin' cattle on the range,
n' I sure hope that it don't change.

THE OLD BUNKHOUSE

Way back when I was just a kid
still wet behind the ears.
Got me a job bustin' broncs
through tough times n' some tears.

The outfit was the old Bar X
owned by a cranky pioneer.
His horses were big n' rank
so I can't remember the year.

What I remember is the old bunkhouse
I can still see it today.
The hands I met, the stories told,
was quite an expose'.

It was our home that old log place,
our shelter from wild dark storms.
It had it's own decor n' grace,
it kept us safe and warm.

The bunkhouse smelled of saddle leather
n' sweat n' grub a cookin' by the fire.
I loved the smell of that old place
It was mighty western in it's own attire.

I'd lay awake at night
n' listen to em' tell,
their great stories of the west
n' of the ridin' they'd done so well.

When the candle would flicker n' die
I'd close my eyes and dream awhile.
In my dreams I could see em' ride,
n' rope n' cowboy up with a big ol' smile.

I really loved that old bunkhouse,
for awhile it was home to me.
But the best thing about the old place
was the cowboy company.

Years later I went back ta' the old Bar X
to see what I could see.
As I approached the old bunkhouse,
I felt that cowboy hospitality.

For a moment I heard the old hands tellin'
their wild ol' tales of the west.
I pushed the squeaky door open
n' all I saw was darkness at best.

I went inside through the sunlight,
through the sunbeams by the door.
But all there was were memories.
Memories I'll hold dear, forevermore!

COWBOY'S WORD

A cowboy's life is a simple life,
he holds ta' that ya' know.
He'll take good care of the cattle
in summer heat or 40 below.

He loves his horses n' the prairie
n' rivers n' mountains high.
He loves ta' watch an eagle fly
in the lofty big blue sky.

The cowboy, he's a simple man,
seems ta' be made of steel.
He's a special caring man,
n' you can bet he's real.

He takes good care of animals
while ridin' on the range.
He takes good care of his family
n' I can tell ya' that won't change.

This cowboy life is pretty tough,
as he works in any weather.
In lightning n' thunder
he'll gather the herd together.

His word is his bond
n' he'll stick by you.
The cowboy is a fine ol' boy.
I can tell ya', "he's tried n' true!

D.C.Decker   Cowboy Word Painter....

A STAMPEDE OF LEARNIN'

When I was still a kid
those many years ago.
I wanted to be a top hand;
there was much I didn't know.

I could ride a horse
n' yell at cattle.
Owned my own gear
n' had a brand new saddle.

I recon ya' could say
I thought I knew it all....
This old timer rode up ta' me,
says, "kid hear my call".

Ya' don't know a damned thing,
about herdin' cattle son.
Ya' got some good potential boy
but don't keep em' on the run.

Before ya' start a runnin' em'
n' thinkin' you're a hand;
start a stampede of learnin'
'cause son I know ya' can.

In all my days upon the range
I took the old mans advice.
One day I finally made a hand
n' thanked him mighty nice.

Last night as I lay on the prairie
n' looked at the stars in the sky,
I could feel the old man's spirit
way up in the sweet by and by.

As I got quiet and listened,
"Son," I heard him say.
"You've made a good hand,
n' I'm right proud of you today."

D.C.Decker......... Humble Cowhand

REAL COW FOLKS
KNOW

Real cowfolks know
there is only one success.
To be able to spend
your life in your own way
is the only real bliss.
To live out in the open space
n' demand ta' be yourself.
It's good ta' give to others
n' treat your horse real fine
and put the demands of others
high upon a shelf.
True western freedom
is unique in all the world.
So pardner hold fast to it
no matter what you do.
For in your own uniqueness
the character of the west
is held true in you!

D.C.Decker....... Cowboy Philosopher
Humble Word Painter

COWBOY'S WORK IS NEVER DONE

They say woman's work is never done.
I recon that's sure true.
But a cowboy's life is as hard as that
n' ya' sure gotta give him his due.

The jolly cowboy is up with the sun
n' saddles em' up ya' see.
He swings his rope n' jingles his spurs
a romantic cowboy is he.

He works all day and half the night
ridin' the lone prairie.
He ropes a steer when it draws near,
for a fine ol' roper is he.

The women's work seems never done
n' these cowboys take time ta' play.
But when the ol' cowherd calls
you can bet he's on his way.

It's not what it's cracked up ta' be,
this romantic cowboy life.
You'll find a hell of a lot of cow manure
n' a hell of a lot of strife.

So ya' greenhorns don't think it's easy
ta' be a cowboy anymore.
'Cause if ya' come home stinkin'
yer woman might run ya' out the door.

She'll tell ya' how she's been a workin'
ever since ya' left.
But all in all if she hugs ya'
ya' know that she's the best.

I know that workin's important
on the ranches way out west.
But it's strong love for each other
that'll let us stand the test!

DC Decker......

33

OLD TIMER SAYS

This old timer don't know
what's happenin' today.
Seems ta' be yurself n' be uncommon
is not an acceptable way.
Somebody is a tryin'
ta' make everybody the same.

Ya' gotta be like peas in a pod
if you're gonna fit their game.
What's become of the good ol' folks
who hang on to their heritage?
Are they goin' by the wayside
like the old horse drawn carriage?

Ol' friend don't let em' do it.
Stand up an raise a fit.
For all the richness of the west
took a mighty bunch of misfits.
It took courage ta' make America great.
Lets not get common or second rate.

Vel Miller

Hold your western heritage, ride it clean and true.
Be yurself, make a stand, no matter what ya' do.
For all the pioneers of yesterday
keep ridin' the true western way.
Hold on to the good things of our past
n' ride hard so we can make 'em last.

Folks, don't let 'em numb ya' down
n' take your dignity n' your western crown.
Be your different self in all you do,
'cause pardner we all need you.
Stand up n' ride tall,
'cause the old west needs ya' one and all!

D.C. Decker.............
Lover of the West
Humble Word Painter

JUST' A COWBOYIN'

It was early mornin'
before the sun came up.
It was goin' ta' be a long day,
miles ta' ride, goin' ta' be tough.

The boss had me ridin' the big circle
in this country, wild n' rough.
Me n' ol' hoss were done eatin'
so I lead em' ta' the water trough.

Cowboy life seemed ta' lose it's glory
when the sky turns cold n' grey.
But when ya' see God's creation
it'll warm yer heart each day.

As I rode out that mornin'
a great message came through.
This cowboy life's a blessin'
n' ta' cowboyin' I'll stay true.

Whatever cowboyin' ya' have ta' do,
no matter what kind of day;
no matter what the hardships,
you've chosen a mighty fine way.

Maybe ya' won't go down as some hero
or scholar, or president or king.
But ya' will have that great freedom
of cowboyin' n' doin' yer own thing.

Be thankful fer livin' in God's nature,
bein' close ta' the soil where cattle go.
Ridin' o'er mountains n' prairies
with rivers n' creeks below.

Just ta' ride in the wild west country
with it's history of hoof, hide n' horn,
n' ta' be ridin' yer favorite hoss
should make ya' feel glad ya' was born.

Cowboy Word Painter.......   D.C. Decker

UP BEFORE DAYLIGHT

It was still dark out
as I pulled my bedroll back.
Had ta' check the remuda
n' reach n' get my cache.

Ol' Cookie was up a bangin' his pans,
damned near scared me ta' death.
He was makin' coffee in the dark
it smelled right good, I guess.

The horses were shakin' off the dust
from a rollin' on the ground.
Thought it was a comin' daylight
but not fer a few hours I found.

Ol' Cookie was a makin' breakfast
n' then he rang his bell.
He made bacon n' hotcakes n' eggs n' all,
the things he made so well.

The buckeroos n' cowhands gathered
in the darkness of the morn.
It was a cowboy custom
ever since a cowman was born.

They sat around n' ate a bunch
n' smoked, n' drank a gall-on.
They talked around the warm morning fire
n' sat there with their hats on.

Then they'd fumble round in the dark
tryin' ta' saddle a wild one.
In the dark ya' could hear em' cuss a lot
tryin' ta' find their way some.

Those old hands were dedicated
in keepin' with the west, I swear.
They had ta' get a goin' before dawn;
before the sun chased the cold night air.

The early mornin' gatherin'
was special in it's own way.
It was time ta' talk of cowboy things
n' ta' buddy up that day!

D.C. Decker..
Ol' Cowboy Word Painter

COWBOY STORIES & DREAMS

THIS PART IS ABOUT COWBOYS
N' THEIR FEELIN'S. SOME OF YOU
MIGHT REMEMBER YOUR OWN
HEARTFELT FEELIN'S ABOUT
THESE THINGS.......

A COWBOY'S MOTHER

Ya' know a cowboys mother
is as special as can be.
'Cause cowboys are the
independent ones ya' see.
God knew these children
would need a special kind
ta' provide a guiding hand.
Some one ta' share
the joy and care,
ta' help and understand-
Cowboys, if the truth
were really known,
needs someone whose
love and deep concern,
would keep a growin'
year by year.
N' that's why God made
cowboy's mothers,
so wonderful n' dear.......

D.C. Decker.. Cowboy Philosopher & Word Painter

Hold your mother dear! For if
you think she is gone; you're
wrong. Her spirit and thoughts
are with you for eternity............

COWBOY KID'S RAINSTORM

THE CHORES WERE DONE
I FILLED THE TANK
THE BARN DOORS SHUT
I GAVE IT A YANK.

THE LIVESTOCK'S BEEN FED
CLEANED UP THE JUNK
WALKED THROUGH THE BARNYARD
WAS THERE I SUNK.

HEADED TO THE BUNKHOUSE
TO GET SOME DRY SOCKS
GOT ALMOST TO THE DOOR
N' SLIPPED ON A BIG OL' ROCK.

A HELL OF A TIME
IN THIS POURING RAIN
WAS NEEDIN' MY SLICKER
OH! WHAT A PAIN.

AFTER SLIPPIN' N' SLIDDIN'
I NEEDED A REST.
O' DAMN THAT OL' SLICKER
I'LL JUST WEAR MY VEST.

COMES A HELL OF A DOWN POUR
I'M SLOPPIN' ROUND AT BEST
SURE IS A LOT OF FUN
OUT HERE IN THE WEST.

YOUNG D.C. DECKER........................

Vel Miller

42

KEEP THE WEST ALIVE

It's a great gift of GOD
the American West.
I feel it slippin' away.
We need to hold on
n' give it our best,
Lord knows we all love the west.

Progress they call it, a changin' of time.
Like a lantern that's losin' it's gleam.
A sad day I call it, our heritage slippin'
when time is a stealin' my dreams.
The culture n' heritage must be preserved
n' it's greatness should not be disturbed.

As for me I'll continue to ride the range
dreamin' of cowboys n' broncos n' sage.
I'll go on livin' the old west
'cause frankly that's what I do best.
I'll hold on n' do my part
n' be with the ones who knows my heart.

In all the world there is just one American West with all it's splendor. It's romantic history and the many characters, both young and old, who shaped it's distinct culture brought to this country a very special place in the annuals of the world. I thank everyone who in their own way contribute to the preservation of this most magnificent culture.

Word Painter
Lover of the West
Horse Whisperer   D.C. Decker

43

WORN OUT BOOTS

Twas' late in the fall, the roundups were o'er,
needed ta' ride n' find a new chore.
Was wantin' ta' get on with a big outfit this time.
I'd rode with the rest,
now I was wantin' the best.

When I'd ride up ta' the headquarters on the next ranch
they'd judge me fer sure by the cut of my pants.
They'd look me over from my brim ta' my boots.
If your outfit they admired,
you could bet you'd get hired.

I recon we looked like a top hand except for one thing,
my old boots had big holes plumb through the soles.
My boots were a sight to behold.
Not only were the soles worn through,
the vamps were worn out too.

I'd been ta' the Frazer Saddlery just last year,
got me a new rig, a pair of chaps n' some gear.
I really enjoyed that ol' place.
The stuff was right good, the cost quite dear
I throwed my saddle on ol' Grey n' rode up here.

My spurs are good un's, from the prison at Canon City.
I was lookin' good except fer my boots; not so pretty.
How could I impress em' fer a job?
I needed ta' ride up ta' old Cheyenne
before next springs hirin' began.

That winter I rode clear into Cheyenne,
looked up ol' Gus Blucher, he was a fine boot man.
In all the west many say he was the best.
Ol' Blucher could make me a pair,
n' all the hands said he'd be fair.

44

He measured me up n' made a last
built em' tough n' made em' fast.
They were a mighty fine pair of cowboy boots.
The cost was a big $27.50,
Sure as hell I was broke in a jiffy.

Now the word was spread fer miles around,
if a man rode a Frazer n' wore Bluchers he was sound.
The other thing I heard em' say;
if he was ridin' on a good grey,
he could surely ask for more pay.

Even though I was now plumb broke
a buyin' all that gear.
Not knowin' how I'd get my next meal;
I was ridin' high n' full of cheer,
n' I'd get the best of jobs this comin' year.

Winter passed, I made it ya' see.
Proud I rode up ta' the headquarters of the Bar 7T.
The boss looked up n' down n' then he smiled at me.
You sure got good trappin's son n' that's all well n' good,
but can ya' ride n' rope n' herd em' like a top hand should?

D.C. Decker......Cowboy Horse Whisperer n' Ranch Hand

Blucher Boot Co.
"Where Boot Making Is An Art"

DC Decker
Box 777
Pueblo, Colorado

Dear Mr. Decker

We have already finished your fine pair of Blucher boots. It has been difficult to get hold of you. I have sent three penny post cards telling you that your boots are ready. You seemed to be in a big hurry for them. I hope this letter finds you well and that it gets to you.

Sincerly,

Gus Blucher   Cheyenne, Wyoming

They never
lose a Stirrup

--- Shopmade expressly for you from the bench to your feet ---
--- Since 1915 ---

46

COWBOY HEROS

Cowboys have been my heros ever since I was a kid.
To me they were the West's real romance
in everything they did.
When I was young it was hard ta' see em',
but I did my very best.
You see, it was unfortunate
'cause I wasn't born in the West.
Some things I learned early in life,
like bein' good at ridin' a horse.
I'd still have ta' learn ta' rope
n' brand em' up of course.

47

Well friend, I left the city
n' the East as early as I could.
Don't recon it was any surprise ta' my kin,
'cause they all knew I would.
When I got my boots n' spurs n' headed out
I was still wet behind the ears.
Took the train ta' the end of the tracks,
got off in silence, no one ta' greet me, no cheers.
I picked up my bag of belongin's n' started walkin'
but I sure didn't know where.
I spotted this tall lanky cowboy
a standin' over there.

I walked right up n' told em' who I was
n' that I had no place ta' stay.
He sized me up n' then he smiled,
come on son, ya' can go my way.
"I recon ya' wanta be a cowboy,
I can tell, you boys often do.
Ya' want this romantic life
n' ya' want yer freedom too!
Well son, I hope you'll make a cowboy
but let me set the record straight.
You'll ride n' rope alright
n' you'll open and close many a gate."

"Now son let me tell ya' it ain't easy,
ya' can bet your hat on that.
If you become a bronc peeler
they can buck you off right flat.
If you're taken care of cows
at brandin' time thar's a lot of sweat n' dirt.
A cowboy's life is plumb dangerous
n' many a good hand gets hurt.
A cowboy's life is fine for those who know it's ways.
Son, if ya' still wanna be a cowboy, n' I'm sure ya' do,
I'll take ya' on young tenderfoot
n' teach the best ta' you.

D.C Decker................. Cowboy Word Painter

BEFORE FENCES

I don't recon ya' all can remember
way back in the good old days.
We'll it wasn't so glamorous,
it was tough in many ways.

Ranchin' n' cowboyin' took a man
with a damned hard twist,
way back in the good old days
when fences didn't exist.

At roundups n' rodeos
the goin' was mighty hard.
The life was rough
I'm a tellin' ya' pard.

But life had it's glamorous side
like all day bein' horseback
n' chasin' cows on track
n' ropin' em' n' pullin' slack.

Ya' worked from dawn ta' dusk
a workin' in the dirt.
Ya' never even had the time
ta' change yer dirty shirt.

Barbed wire was a nasty thing
when it first came along.
But before barbed wire, ta' chase a cow
fer months ya' might be gone.

Pard, the circles were mighty wide back then
before the fences came.
But I'd druther ride big circles
than ta' work on fencin' in the rain.

Seems cowboyin' was really great
before those damned fences came.
I loved ta' ride the range, back then
I loved the cowboy game.

Ol' D.C. Decker   Ol' Puncher n' Word Painter

THE OLD RANCH

One day when I was a dreamin',
a thinkin' n' a schemin'
I thought I'd ride on back
ta' the old ranch in the blackjack,
so I loaded up my pack.

Twas' 'bout a forty mile ride
n' I rode it all with pride.
I was born on that old place,
lived through hot summers with grace
n' cold winters with the wind in my face.

Memories were comin' with every step.
runnin' behind I thought I saw Ol' Shep.
We rode up ta' the old corral
lookin' for a part of my past
that would boost my ole morale.

Rode up ta' the old ranch house,
It was quiet as a mouse.
Used ta' work n' go on hunts
here on this ol' place.
Sure was a fine outfit, once.

I looked around then gave a yell.
Mighty sad, the place had gone ta' hell.
Big barn was gone, burnt up in a fire,
It had stayed with us long enough
for my ol' dad ta' retire.

Mom, loved this ol' place very much,
worked hard ta' give it a lovin' touch.
We lived here a good long time
n' mom was the soul of this place,
but we lost her in her prime.

I recon things move on quite fast
n' not even dreams can last
I'll leave my past ans sorrows
behind at the ranch this time
n' ride on into my tomorrows.

'Cause if I keep comin' back again
won't know what my future might have been.
Must ride on now n' start a makin' hay
so I can make the best of each n' every day,
n' not let yesterday get in my way.

D.C. Decker.......................   Ol' Rancher

LONE COWBOY'S CHRISTMAS

I rode alone that Christmas Eve
checkin' cattle in the snow
I recon it was 10 below.

It was lonesome out there
a ridin' the range.
I could sure do for a change.

The cattle were still a bawlin',
the hay truck had gone.
I started ta' sing this ol' Xmas song.

I'm a singin' along, jus' me an my hoss,
was a real dark night
but the moon was still in sight.

All of a sudden a red sleigh appeared,
it was such a sight
on this cold an windy night.

Somethin' was wrong, I could see at a glance,
the old Christmas story
had lost some of it's glory.

There in the snow the sleigh came a runnin'
the reindeer were missin',
but the old model T Ford was a hissin'.

A smilin' old man with whiskers, not a beard
came chuggin' up with a sleigh that looked weird.
He was jolly n' laughin' n' that's when I heard.

The spirit of Christmas is not what you get,
it's the spirit of giving
that makes life worth livin'.

The old man n' I jus' looked at the sky,
wonderin' about that old by n' by.
We knew we'd soon say goodbye.

All of a sudden we saw in the sky
a great big star a shinnin' bright.
The Star of David had shown in the night.

Now we were happy, the star shown its might,
MERRY CHRISTMAS TO ALL!
AND TO ALL A GOOD NIGHT!

D.C. Decker.................

OUT MONTANEE WAY

I remember once so long ago
out old Montanee way.
We were all workin' the herd
n' brandin'cattle that day.

The hands were workin' hard
sweatin' n' a stinkin' like a goat.
When this fancy carriage pulls up
this Englishman steps out n' starts ta' gloat.

Well ain't he fancy I says ta' myself
with his two women fine.
N' one when she looked out her bonnet
was uglier than sin, I wouldn't want her fer mine.

The older women was a holdin' her nose
like she didn't like the smell.
She was sure stuck up that's what I suppose
n' by the look on her face you'd think she'd seen hell.

I recon it wasn't proper fer a lady
ta' be out on a Montanee ranch,
with cowboys rough n' ready,
I recon they were takin' a chance.

But the hands were all quite respectful
'til the gentleman looked down his nose.
Then the cowboys got a little playful
n' started playin' with his second hand rose.

A few went over ta' the women
as they got up from their brandin'.
They laughed n' began ta' hug em',
they were all a mighty stinkin'.

If you folks from England are goin' ta' be happy here
get down n' be of good cheer.
You'll have ta' come down off yer high horse,
'cause this is the west my man, sit down n' have a beer.

Ya' could see the stiffness go out of em'
as the women began ta' laugh n' giggle.
They were havin' fun by then
n' the gals began ta' wiggle.

The old Englishman reached into his carriage
he was reachin' fer a gun.
"The best man here will have my daughter in marriage
I'm your new boss so nobody better run."

"I own this Montana ranch now and all the Hereford
cattle.
My Lizbeth wants a cowboy and I don't want a battle."
He looked at me, "First we'll have a wedding here!"
I looked at Lizbeth's face again n' ran jus' like a deer.

I rode fast, clean out past Livingston
so I could get away.
I never went back ta' see those folks
'cause they scared me ta' death that day!

D.C. Decker.....   Cowboy Word Painter

COWBOY LOVIN'

THIS MIGHT BE THE MOST
IMPORTANT POETRY IN THE
BOOK FOR THE REAL ROMANTICS
OF THE WEST. IT MAY INCLUDE
EVERY COWBOY AND COWGIRL
ON THE PRAIRIES, MOUNTAINS
AND VALLEYS. ROMANCE IS A
PART OF THE VAST AND
BEAUTIFUL WEST. LET'S SEE
WHAT THIS OL' COWBOY HAS TO
SAY ABOUT IT. THE ROMANCE OF
THE WEST IS DEEP. IT COVERS
MANY THINGS.

TO MY COWGIRL

My sweet darlin' cowgirl
I do believe that God above
created you for me to love.
He picked you out from all the rest
'cause He sure knew I'd love you best.
I once had a heart called mine tis' true,
now it's gone from me to you.

My cowgirl of the plains,
Take care of it as I have done,
for now you have two n' I have none.
If you go ta' heaven n' I'm not there,
darlin' paint my name on the golden stair.
But ol' lovin' hoss partner,
If I'm not there by judgement day;

You'll know I've gone the other way.

D.C. Decker....... *Cowboy Word Painter*

Ridin' Together

LIVED & LOVED

This ol' cowboy has lived n' loved.
He sure can't deny it.
If you haven't yet my friend
ya' oughta try it.
I have sung n' I have danced
I've smiled n' I have wept.
I have won n' wasted treasure,
I've had my share of pleasure.
Been through a mite of weariness
n' a bunch of dreariness.
I've felt that old emptiness
n' more than my share of pain.
But if you can truly love again,
nothing is in vain.

D.C. Decker..................Lover of life

ARE YOU LOVIN' ME

Sometimes, as I ride the trail of life
n' think of my heart that's true,
I'm a wonderin', if you're lovin' me
like I'm a lovin' you.

Oh! girl am I just dreamin' on
just to take a fall?
Or baby are you lovin' me
"cause I love you best of all.

In all of lifes struggles
there is nothing worse
than a one sided love affair
'cause it's a painful curse.

So darlin' I really need to know
n' I need ya' ta' tell it true.
Are you still a lovin' me
like I'm a lovin' you?

D.C. Decker .... Romantic Word Painter

COWBOY'S NIGHT

I've seen enough big city lights
n' big ole city sights.
I just crave the peaceful nights
under a western moon.
Lookin' up at the big ol' sky
with the horses n' my gal n' I.

We'll sit in the light of a big full moon
n' I'll sing her a cowboys tune.
It'll be a beautiful night
right in the middle of June.
We'll talk of love n' summertime
n' that we might get married soon!

D.C. Decker........Cowboy Dreamer

COWBOY JOHNNY WALKER

There was a good ol' cowboy
he could rope n' ride.
Sure he was a good hand
but he didn't have much pride.

You bet he was an all-around cowboy
but he took ta' drinkin' bad.
He left his family for the bars,
in all it was most sad.

His wife sent in a letter
which Johnny Walker read.
Please come home to me,
I love you, n' the children need fed.

Ol' Johnny Walker pulled his face up
from his namesake on the bar.
He saw his ol' face in the bar mirror,
it set his mind ajar.

Then he saw this vision,
his cryin' wife in tattered clothes,
The children hungry n' sad,
n' what else no one knows.

He reached again for Johnny Walker Red
when another vision turned to him.
He was layin' in the gutter
his chances mighty slim.

He pulled his hand back from his namesake,
raised the letter to his eyes n' read again.
Johnny Walker please come home
can't you feel our pain?

He got up n' staggered to his feet,
sure was headin' out the door.
Johnny was determined to get back home
and graze the bars no more.

If you had read the whole letter
that Johnny Walker read,
your heart would break too n'
you'd never touch another drop.

OF JOHNNY WALKER RED.....................

D.C. Decker .... Cowboy Word Painter

COWBOY'S SWEETHEART

I don't know where you're ridin' today,
sure hope it's a safe n' happy place.
I love ya' sweet cowgirl wherever ya' ride,
always good blessin's n' a smile on your face.
May ya' get yer good wishes
I know they'll come true.
Honey, I hope you're true ta' me
like I'm true ta' you.
I yearn for the days
when we won't be apart.
'Cause my sweet cowgirl
you're always in my heart!

DC. Decker

Romantic Word Painter

BECAUSE YOU LOVE ME

I've been kind of a loser
in my wild cowboy ways
Hangin' in bars n' bein' a bum,
I've sure had some tough old days.
Honey, because ya' love me, I have found
new joys that were not mine before.
New stars have lighted up the night time sky
with glorious mornings o'er n' o'er.
Because ya' love me I can rise
to spiritual heights n' peaceful power.
My cowgirl, because ya' love me I can learn
the highest use of every hour.
Because ya' love me,
it sure helps an amazin' lot,
'Cause now my love, I have a reason
to give it all I've got!

D.C. Decker

LOVE THEM COWGIRLS

All of us ol' cowboys
love them cowgirls a lot.
When we see em' in their tight pants
we get a little hot.

I recon dresses were better
they didn't show so much.
But hell, it's hard ta' ride a horse
when your so out of touch.

I recon those old side saddles
were OK in their time.
But it's damned hard ta' rope n' ride
with both legs on one side.

Now we love them sweet ol' cowgirls
ta' dance with now n' then.
'Cause cowboys have been a dancin'
with them gals since way back when.

Ya' know them pretty cowgirls
have come a long, long way.
They can drive them pickup trucks
n' do the chores all day.

They can love ya' n' be with ya',
n' they can stand the test.
N' boys let me tell ya',
they're the best thing in the west!

D.C. Decker.... Cowboy Lovin' Word Painter

MY OL' WOMEN & ME

This is a story poem. I've seen it happen. This ol' boys been beat on more than once. You can bet it's one of those deals were it is so much fun makin' up after the wreak. Hope none of you folks ever knew somethin' like this. It could be hard on your health n' well-bein' .... But we love em' just the same.

My ol' women n' me
got cabin fever in December.
It was the longest winter
I can remember.

Sure was long, n' cold as hell,
the ride ta' town was rough as can be,
with a winter blizzard
blowin' right at me.

I recon I should have stayed at the cabin
a rockin' by the firelight.
But I was a wantin' ta' get me a drink
'cause my women n' I had a big ole fight.

I rode clear into my favor rite bar
n' tied my grey hoss ta' a tree.
The snow was gettin' mighty deep,
came over my boots plumb up ta' my knee.

The place was nearly empty
at the Honkey Tonk Saloon.
It was damned sure dirty
like it never saw a broom.

I walked across the old wood floor
n' got up on my stool.
I'll not let her get the best of me,
I'm as stubborn as a mule.

The bartender came over to me.
"Give me five," I told the man.
"No, five whiskeys you fool,"
as he reached ta' shake my hand.

He set up five along the bar
n' nary said a word.
He set up five more, with cigarette in his mouth
he mumbled, but couldn't be heard.

It took all day n' half the night
ta' get twenty glasses down.
Was damned sure fogettin' my troubles
as the room went round n' round.

I recon night time had come on
at the Honky Tonk Saloon.
Now the place was plumb empty
n' I'd been settin' a way past noon.

The shot glasses were a lined up plenty,
the old juke box was playin' Hank Snow.
It was mighty lonely n' I was mighty drunk
if ya' really want ta' know.

Finally, the ol' boy behind the bar
says, "cowboy you gotta go!"
When I said, "Hell ya' say,"
he threw me out in the snow.

I climbed up on old Greyboy
as drunk as a cowboy can be.
The ride in darkness n' snow
ta' the cabin was dangerous ya' see.

If I fell off in a snow bank
folks might never have known.
Er' if old Greyboy bucked me off
n' broke my bones, I'd never get home.

But let me tell ya' folks, that would be easy
compared ta' the cabin war.
'cause my ol' lady would beat me
n' I'd be totally sore.

Well folks, these storms would be calms
compared ta' the cabin storm.
I recon my ol' women will kill me
n' there won't be a soul ta' mourn.

I was ridin' home on this damned cold night
tryin' ta' sober up in the wind.
Should I tell her I got lost
er' tell her where I've been.

It was a comin' mornin'
when I put ol' grey away.
I'll tell her that I love her
so I can live another day.

As I opened the door ta' our cabin
she was standin' there waitin' fer me.
She flung her arms around my neck
n' said, "My man don't cha leave me."

"I'm sorry dear about the fight,
I love you so much," she said.
"Come on darlin', my dear man
let's hug n' go ta' bed!"

So folks, don't take things fer granted,
take time ta' talk em' out.
Be honest with each other,
don't just run around n' pout.

D.C. Decker   **Life Word Painter & Cowboy Poet**

COWGIRL SOUL MATE SONG

To Gloria with Love,

```
      E                          G
I can tell by the look in your  eyes.
   G    A                E
I can  tell by the smile on your face.
      E                      G
You're the  one I have searched for  forever.
    G       A            E
You're the  one who's soul mates with mine....To Chorus I
         E
       You're the one,   you're the one
                         G
       the one I've searched   for.
        G     A                    E
       Yes it's   you, soul mate love of  mine.
         E                     G
       O' Soul mate of mine I knew I'd    love you!
        G    A              E
       You've   been forever on my    mind.
   E                        G
    O' soul mate of mine I'll never leave    you.
    G       A                     E
It took a   life time to find where you    were.
      E               E     G
Now we can live love  dear    forever, cause
    G     A                   E
I've   found you soul mate love of mine.........(soft.

      E                          G
When you're near I feel so com    plete dear....(soft
   G   A                      E
We   know what's said without a   whisper..
   E                G
Our world is finally   together.
    G                       E
O' Soul mate in harmony we'll   live!!!!
```

Ending with chorus 2nd........

To my wife Gloria from the ol' cowboy composer DC..........

72

SPIRIT COWBOY WORD PAINTER

THESE POEMS COME NOT SO
MUCH FROM HEART, AS SOUL.
THEY REFLECT MY FEELINGS
FROM A PLACE OF SPIRIT; THE
INNER-CONNECTED ASPECTS OF
FINE PEOPLE AND THEIR
GREATNESS I CALL SPIRIT.
MANKIND'S MOST IMPORTANT
PART, OUR SPIRIT.

OL' COWBOY'S PRAYER

Forgive me Lord, when sometimes I forget,
You know the reasons that are hid.
You understand the things that hurt me so.
You know me better than my mother did.

Lord, right me at times when I turn aside.
On this long trail of life be my Guide.
Help me grow n' help me know;
How to get to Your great Divide..............

D.C. Decker........   **Spirit Word Painter**

I read a poem like this when I was very young. The poet was unknown. I have taken the chance that he would not mind my changes as I cannot remember his exact words. I sure would have liked to have known him.   DCD.............

WHAT IS MY TASK?

Ol' friend, don't forget n' you must know,
you have a life n' you gotta go.
Ol' pardner, some things in life,
are important ta' know,
if by chance ya' want ta' grow.

What is my task?   I need not ask,
to love someone more dearly is my task.
To help a wandering child to find their way.
To ponder noble thoughts and pray.
And love my GOD with all my heart today!

Father, thank you for keeping Your name in my heart!
With Your name I'll never part.
Whatsoever I sow, that shall I also reap.
I'll do my duty, I'll do my task,
My hearts on You, so I need not ask.

D.C. Decker

Spirit Word Painter

LOOKING IN

With tears running, O' Great Spirit -
    Looking in with running eyes,
    I see the tree has never fully bloomed.
Almost a pitiful old man you see me here.
    I have fallen away and have done nothing.
Here at the center of my world,
    where You took me when I was very young,
    and You taught me.
Here old, now I stand
    and the tree has withered.
Great Spirit I recall the great vision You sent me.
    Where has the Eagle gone?
    How then is my tree?
It may be that some little root of the sacred tree
    still lives.
Nourish it then, O' Great spirit,
    that it may leaf and bloom
    and be filled with singing birds.
Come to me again, O' Great Spirit,
    so this tree will bloom and flourish
    and provide shelter for many
    before I cross over to You!

      D.C. Decker   _spirit word painter_

GREAT SPIRIT

Hear this ol' puncher
who is, I recon over the hill.
Listen to his voice,
if you only will.

The Most Great Spirit
who created all you see.
He gives you all ya' need
so ya' can be all you can be.

Pardner, He gives us each mornin'
the brightness n' the sun.
He gives us laughter ta' share
n' good chores to be done.

He has given us rainbows,
n' flowers n' song
n' the hands of dear friends
that come n' help us along.

He's given us mighty prayer
with all it's great power.
It lightens our hearts
in our troubled hour.

Ol' western friends,
He has given us mighty blessin's
to brighten up our way
n' always brings so many gift's
In the dawning of each day!!!!

D.C. Decker.............   **Spirit Word Painter**

LITTLE COWGIRL
SHERIDAN

Up on the mountain
that special day
a little girl was born
in a natural way.
Her grandpa said
a special prayer
for her that day
that GOD would care for her
n' her mommy n' daddy too!
And HE will grant her
the blessing's
of HIS love
her whole life through.............

To: Sheridan from grandpa

D.C. Decker...... spirit word painter

June 12, 1996

79

LITTLE COWBOY SEES

I see You, I see You!
cried the little cowboy.

I see You in this morning sky,
he cried with joy!

I see You when the birds fly by
yes, I see You in the big blue sky.

I see You in that tree over there
gee whiz, God I see You everywhere.

Children are such a great delight
for they still see in purest light.

They are yet free from dominance,
are not filled with contaminates.

They are fresh as first light of day,
they can see a brighter way.

Children would stay in pureness light,
if adults would not condemn their wondrous flight.

D.C. Decker .... <u>Lover of children</u>

OLD COWBOY'S SOUL

My soul grieves a bunch today.
I've failed myself
n' others too!
My old grievin' soul, what shall I do?

Repent of course, Repent they say,
else we'll all shun ya' on this day.
The hell they say, just listen to God's will
His love for you will be greater still.

Folks say, we'll leave ya' alone
so you can atone.
Yer life's a mess,
you've failed the test.

God, O' God, please hear my plea,
I beg of You don't leave me!
"O' son of Mine, they are not your judge,
I know your soul, I will not budge."

This old cowboy's soul is better now,
it changed in the spirit somehow.
Friend, don't listen to what people say,
know yourself, n' you'll find the way.

If you need a partner, He's the main One.
You'll never walk alone.
Just as you love Him, you'll be alright,
n' soon He'll give you back your light!

D.C. Decker............ Cowboy spirit man

TEACH US

Wakan Tanka, Almighty Creator,
wonderful Father of us all.

Our hearts are buried
in the dust and debris of wrong!

Teach us to unbury our hearts
from all the prejudice around it.

Teach us to unbury our hearts
from all the hatred around it!

Teach us to unbury our hearts
from our demands of separation from You.

Teach us to unbury our hearts
from this nasty prison of self.

Teach us the True Spiritual World
so we can know Your True Reality!

Teach us the True Spiritual World
so we can love all peoples!

Teach us the True Spiritual World
so we can enjoy the grace of unity!

Teach us the True Spiritual Reality
so we can know the joy of living.

So our souls can grow in this knowledge
Almighty GOD please teach us!

D.C. "Kicking Horse" Decker...... Spirit Talker..

Always Learning – Teach Us!

NEW DAY DAWNED

Mankind must now replace
    oppression and killing
        with helping and living.

The degradation that has persisted
    through centuries must cease
        the wish of the world is lasting peace.

Each person must stop acting about life
    as a battle to be won by force.
        We have important work to do, of course.

In harmony we should do our job
    to help each other just in time
        for the progress and maturing of
    humankind.

The steadfast concerns for truth and reality
    a kind and loving tenacity
        bring perseverance for a better society.

The hearts, minds, and consciousness
    of all the world should see
        this would bring us all together in Harmony!

So all you pardners do your part
'cause ya' know this from the start.
It's time ta' go back ta' the Code of the West
n' it's time ta' act from your heart.
Put out some effort ta' do your best,
we've all been blessed, we can pass the test!

D.C. Decker...   <u>Word Painter.</u>

THE GREATEST VIRTUE

Ol' pardner, there are many virtues
on this you can depend,
there is one that's tough to mend.

The greatest virtue
of all life's achievements
is victory over oneself.

Those who have fought and won
are truly blessed
for they can never really know defeat.

So as you ride life's trails
it's good to look inside
n' strive n' not compromise!

D.C.Decker.........   spirit word painter

COWBOY TAKE A STAND

Friend, I know life can be difficult
on occasion it has wounded me.
I've taken many a shot
n' my ol' heart grieves.
Many times it's been broken
n' put me on my knees.

Every time that I'll look up
I hear a voice from above.
"You can make it, I have made you,
surely you can beat the strife."
"Come and fly like a loving dove
I will give you the zest for life!"

"You hang in there and you'll remain
to ride tall in the saddle once again.
Get back to your true self,
then you will sustain.
Look inside, your mighty spirit dwells
to carry you on and make you well."

So saddle up your very best horse
n' ride in style n' grace.
You can ride into the wind again,
there's nothin' you can't face.
You can embrace fine natures place
n' soar with eagles on your chase.

You're the one who can make it work,
you're God's child n' not some jerk.
You can create n' love n' give your all.
For once again you're ridin' tall.
If you love God, n' why wouldn't you.
He'll Love you fer sure, I know it's true!!

DC Decker............spirit word painter

PURPOSE & PEACE

FOR COUNTRY FOLKS & CITY SLICKERS TOO!

O' People find your precious purpose,
the exalted reason for your being.
Do not live in heedless stupor,
be of those with virtues caring.

THEN PEACE WILL COME!

O' you souls who are bent on anger,
who's world is in danger.
Until the souls of men are calmed,
until these frenzied hearts lay down,

NO PEACE WILL COME!

O' friends, until these wolves with nashing teeth
become the lambs of God,
until we see true heavens shining up above
until the fires of hatred are quenched by love,

NO PEACE WILL COME!

O' lovers of peace in the quiet of oneness,
until the tyrants foul odor is blown away
by the sweet scents of harmony,
until the darkness turns to light,

NO PEACE WILL COME!

O' lovers of reality find your real place.
No one was born to hate or kill,
not even of another's race!
When prejudice and hatred are our ills,

NO PEACE WILL COME!

O' caring ones please be aware,
we must strive with hearts that trust!
For if we don't we will condemn
our fellowman, to a heap of dust!

NO PEACE WILL COME!

O' lovers you all know the wisdom of His world!
When justice, love and charity bring the perfect power:
THEN PEACE WILL COME AND YOU WILL KNOW THE HOUR!

THIS COWBOY'S MOM

My Mom was a special one,
she taught us well you see.
Among many, many things
we were to be the best we could be.
Things were mighty tough
in those good old days.
She took us to church
and showed us the good ways.
She was a precious mother
but God took her home.
In the prime of her life
she got sick, no more to roam.
No one knows the silent heartaches
I have faced alone.
Only those who have lost can tell
of the grief born in silence
for a mom we loved so well.
With a smile on my face,
amidst pleasures I was blue.
In time the heartache eases,
Mom, we're still missing you!

D.C. Decker......   word painter

Dear Mother Reita,

Although I cannot see you now,
I know that you're still here.
I'll still talk to you,
but in another sphere.
You were just too precious and too fair
for God to trust to mortals care.
HE deemed it wise to take you home
no more pain you'd have to bear.......

Your Loving son,
Donny C.

PARDNER, HAVE YOU EVER

Pardner, have you ever felt the cold n' glistening glaze
of nights eyes as you rode a cold n' lonely trail;
when the last rays of light show only the distant horizon
n' darkness caresses you like a shawl of fear
n' the coolness of night chills you to the bone?

Pardner, have you ever felt the warm n' gentle gaze
of the sun on a cold winters morn;
when the rays of warmth caress your face,
n' the chill of night recedes as the sun smiles down
upon the frosted earth n' gives joy to your soul?

Pardner, have you ever seen the fear n' hate in a soul
that's lost it's way; or the stone cold look upon the face
of mankind that sees no way, with blinded eyes n' bowed down head
n' spirit dead; the lonely chill of fear n' death of those
who see no hope, whose will is gone n' cannot carry on?

Ol' Pardner, have ya' ever known the sadness n' pain
of a heart that's about to break; the turned down lips
n' moistened eyes of someone left alone, wrinkled brow n' turned down face,
the saddened heart that sets apart a life that finds no peace
n' has never found the great comfort in the ONE who created this place?

Well Ol' Pardner, for those who can look n' see, they have found
their joy n' hope, they have found their way each n' every day.
In a gentle touch of mother n' child, the bright eyes n' joyous cries
of children at play, who smile with their whole face, n' look at birds
flying by, way up in the vast blue sky.

Pardner, have you ever seen the sparkle of light in the eyes of age
n' a love that has passed the test of time; have you ever known
the loving embrace of a lover that shines with God's Grace,
or the warmth n' peace of a place you call home, n' the comforting love
of a soulmate n' friend, one who will stick with you to the end?

Ol' Pardner, have you ever known a soul that shines with the passing of time
n' their light helps guide your way; have you ever thought you might be
just that kind of guiding light; that your truth n' love could shine so bright,
with just your smile or your talk for awhile, your kindness n' caring
that someone's cup you might fill up, wouldn't that be daring?

Well Pardner, we all could do it if we would, our days will come
you can rest assured. Ones love n' kindness will find the way
to bring the goodness into play each day; true love can hold everything close n' dear
n' the brightness of the spirit will surely appear. I know you'll see it clear. Ol' Pard,
If you'll ride the CODE of the WEST, I'm sure you'll ride the best!

D.C. Decker .... Cowboy Word Painter

TRUE COUNTRY LIFE

IN THE COUNTRY, AS OPPOSED
TO THE CITY, WE FIND THE REAL
DEPTH OF NATURE IN ALL HER
GLORY. THIS FEELING OF SPACE
AND TIME EXPOSED IN THE
VASTNESS OF MOUNTAIN,
STREAM AND PRAIRIE LENDS TO
THE WONDERFUL SPIRIT OF THE
WEST. I TRY TO PUT SOME OF IT
DOWN AS A COWBOY WORD
PAINTER WOULD. THE WEST;
IT'S GOOD FOR ALL OF US!

94

MOTHER NATURE

If you'll follow Mother Nature's bliss,
not the drought or snakes that hiss.
No, follow the trail you ought to ride
where the grass is tall and the rivers wide.

The bliss of nature waits for you
on a smooth ol' trail, if you only knew.
No matter which pasture you ride today
you should grow in wisdom n' find your way.

You'll enjoy nature's refreshments my country friend,
she'll bring you harmony deep within.
Learn to ride your innate trail of bliss
and give mother nature a big ol' kiss.

Look deep within her, she's alive ya' know.
You can plant the seeds n' she'll make em' grow.
She's so beautiful n' she's forgivin',
so each of us can go on livin'.

Cowboys n' Cowgirls hear this ol' mans call.
Be good n' love her one and all!
As you ride o'er your country she sure makes life grand!
In all her vastness, she gives us a hand!

D.C. Decker

COUNTRY FOLKS LOVE NATURE

Country folks get up early in the morn
to see the sun rise each day.
They see the greatness of nature
in a deep n' glorious way.

They look up n' hope ta' see dark clouds
when the west wind blows.
For in the rain their future lies;
it gives life to everything that grows.

When yer runnin' cattle or raisin' horses,
ya' look at nature with a different view.
In every blade of grass a growin' on the earth
ya' see the miracle of nature seen by just a few.

In all of nature there is no doubt
when the foals n' calves born
n' springtime sprouts anew,
the whole outdoors is sacred, not ta' be torn.

Country folks live right close ta' nature,
they can lean into the mighty winds of strife.
Cause in those winds, n' storms, n' rains
they surely know it all brings life.

So friend, no matter where ya' live
remember the country way.
Learn ta' love Mother Nature
each n' every day!

For she provides for your very life
n' if you're goin' ta' abuse her,
her sacred nature could die in vain
n' friend, you'd sure enough miss her!

D.C. Decker..........Ol' cowboy word painter

THE WESTERN SKY

We were workin' the herd,
it was early fall.
Had ta' round up the cattle
we didn't mind at all.

The circles had been rode,
some stories had been told.
The days gatherin' was done
n' nobodied been out run.

The cattle were penned n' sorted,
been doctored n' inspected.
Was headed up to the headquarters,
when I reined up unexpected.

I was ridin' the flea bit grey
n' lookin' up ta' the sky.
There was just the four of us,
ol' John, n' Button, brother Tom n' I.

We rode up on this grassy knoll,
it was beautiful, ya' all would know.
This beauty caught my eye,
as I looked out n' up at the big ol' sky.

We all reined up ta' take a look
at the great wonder that nature took.
Our ol' dog Cody laid down for a rest,
we were all together; it was the best!

Is there a better life on earth
than this western cowboy way?
We've come ta' surely realize
he sees through different eyes.

He can see God everywhere,
even in big clouds away up there.
He sees his Creator in all nature's things.
n' sometimes he soars as on eagles wings.

You see, the cowboy has it figured out,
what religion is all about.
He feels closer to his Creator,
under the big ol' sky, I have no doubt!

DC Decker.....   <u>Word Painter</u>

DESTINY COWBOY CODE

In all the west
there is this code.
It brings us all together
in our actions, n' makes a mode.

There is a destiny
that makes us brothers.
What we send into the life of
others comes back into our own.

As you ride through life
find the good in others.
Look into yourself n' find
they are truly brothers.

The west is a special place
of hardship n' love.
Make the best of it,
n' seek the one above!

D.C. Decker   word painter....

THE CAMP FIRE

Did ja' ever watch a campfire
n' see the dancin' flames?
There's no better place fer thinkin'
out there on the range.

If yer out there jus' thinkin'
n' not knowin' jus' why,
you'll stay n' stare at the hot coals
n' watch the campfire die.

While lookin' into the fires flames
I saw the past ride by.
N' as I gazed n' felt the heat,
I saw both earth n' sky.

Lookin' at the fires flames
was peaceful as can be.
But when I saw the future
I got down on one knee.

I backed away from the dyin' fire,
my dreams gave me a thrill.
As I backed n' turned in the darkness
the cold night gave me a chill.

I'll watch an ol' campfire
as often as I can
for I'm an old cowpuncher
n' a campfire lover I sure am !!

Wayne Justus, artist

D.C. Decker...... cowboy word painter.

100

TRUE LIFE

Say Partner, before ya' go off the rail,
if you'll follow yer spiritual bliss
n' put yerself on the right trail,
life's a real fine ride, one ya' shouldn't miss.

Get you n' your ol' hoss trackin'
down the trail just meant fer you.
It's been laid down fer yer good
n' you can surely find it too!

Come on, let's ride the trail
we ought to be a livin'.
Wherever you are, grow in wisdom,
follow yer bliss, n' learn by givin'.

When ya' follow yer natural bliss
You'll find it's deep refreshment.
The real life within ya'
can bring so much contentment.

All the stuff that hurts inside,
the junk that causes pain,
can be gone from us so easily,
like a walkin' in the rain.

The power lies in each of us,
 land, n' flowers n' animals to help.
Mother Nature holds the peacefulness,
few answers lie in the social kelp.

Well Pardner, look within yourself,
you'll find how great you are.
You'll find you're good n' true,
you'll find that your a star!

D.C. Decker....   *spirit word painter*

This poem is for everyone. No matter where they are from, what color they
are or even what they believe. God made everyone. Love all people as
thyself...........

WESTERN BEAUTY

Ol' friends, if this story is rightly told
you'll get a glimpse of the beauty of old.
As I ride along in this perpetual spell
I can see and feel it, in nature's signs that tell.

We see this beautiful west when we look up
n' find God's colors in a bloomin' flowers cup.
Gentle breezes speak to us now n' then
n' cause a stir in the minds of men.

The winds that blow my horses mane
carries a coolin' feelin' n' a warm refrain.
This wind that blows the desert sands
is the wind that blows the snow that stands.

When I'm ridin' I can see beauty all relates
to the big old west n' the Paradise Ranch gates.
At this fine ol' ranch the gardens are bright,
scenes long time hidden from sight.

In the canyons are rivers, creeks n' waterfalls,
the waters pure, get a drink while sittin' by the walls.
In the gardens on this ranch you may pluck one rose
who's beauty is beyond belief, that much every one knows.

The river's moving on, now in light, now in shade,
as it winds it's way thru cottonwood trees, n' glade.
Watchin' the stream glide by, I offer many thanks,
thankful for the flowers a bloomin' on these banks.

Got off my horse n' tied em' in some shade
where dark green leaves in sunshine played.
From big rocks n' falls a gentle murmur fell
to my ears like the chimes of a silver bell.

You've heard the sound, God's voice in water's song,
n' the birds make the chorus with their joyful throng.
The river keeps the melody that sounds so fair,
ya' all heard it sure, cause you've been there.

On this ranch the voice of nature calls with a sigh,
it's a voice of our future n' of days gone by.
Leanin' against my horse, with tears of glad surprise
our mother earth n' all she gives, sure makes us rise!

Who has not bowed low at an earthly shrine,
each heart should have its love; God's earth is mine.
I love the horses n' cattle, all in the west pray tell,
but how many loves still hide in my heart's deepest cell.

Like some vision by magic up reared in the night
stood my own fair ranch in the mornin's light.
Not a hammer nor chisel, none but God gave it mold:
it stood so stately like a giant castle of old.

Wake up ol' cowboy, your horse is tied up over there,
come on get on n' get ta' ridin' em' with special care!
The whole west is the Paradise Ranch, rivaled by no one;
 it's the place to love, past the setting of the sun.

Ya' all saddle up yer ponies n' take this ride with me,
 the west holds endless beauty for all of us to see.
 Ya' all should know; this beauty's held by reverence
 please show your respect, it's time for our deliverance.

The west still holds many mysteries, of that we know,
so get on your horse n' ride, brother it's time ta' go!
It holds the nature n' beauty of life, a right spirit shone,
it holds many mysteries of God, n' His I call my own!

D.C. Decker   Spirit Painter

103

LONG NIGHT'S RIDE

The snow was deep, some places belly high.
I'd ridden most all night
I was thinkin' I might die.

It was mighty cold that night
Snow still comin' down.
Was a dark ol' winter's sight.

My hoss was gettin' mighty tired.
In the blizzard n' the snowdrifts
he was gettin' mired.

Our food was gone
n' we were lost
too worn ta' carry on.

Just a cold n' tired cowboy here
ridin' a tired out hoss.
The end was near, that was clear.

No matches to light a fire by,
no warm place ta' call home.
Just me an ol' hoss thinkin' we might die.

Just then we rode by a gatepost
with a ranch sign hangin' there.
All I could do is hope for the most.

In about a hundred yards or so
I spotted a light
through the blinding snow.

I spurred ol' hoss n' made him go
through the snow
toward the fire's glow.

Was an old ranch bunkhouse there
as cozy as can be ya' see.
A warm fireplace n' nice folks who care.

D.C. Decker   Cowboy Word Painter...................

OL' COWBOY PHILOSOPHER

THIS PHILOSOPHY COMES OUT IN THE HEART OF THE PEOPLE OF THE WESTERN COUNTRY. IN MANY CASES IT IS THE SOUL SPEAKIN' FROM THE DEPTH OF LIVIN' ON THE VAST AND RUGGED PLAINS, DESERTS AND MOUNTAIN RANGES OF THAT SPECIAL PLACE IN ALL THE WORLD: THE AMERICAN WEST. IT HAS IT'S OWN UNIQUE SPIRIT. COWBOY WORD PAINTERS AND POETS FEEL IT SO THEY CAN PUT IT DOWN FOR THE AGES TO READ.

COWBOY DREAMER

When I was just a tenderfoot
those many years ago.
I was always a dreamin'
this ya' ought ta' know.

At times I'd talk
'bout my dreams ta' folks.
They'd say, "yer jus' ta' dreamer"
n' that would kill my hopes.

In spite of all
the bad ole ridicule,
I just kept on dreamin'
like a damned ol' fool.

Friend, many of my wildest dreams
came true in my long life.
Mostly the good ones it seems
in among the strife.

Now I'm no spring chicken
just an old man ya' see.
N' I'm still a dreamin' cause
if I wasn't, it wouldn't be me.

Ol' pardner, always have a dream
n' believe it will come true.
Strive ta' make it happen
in everythin' ya' do.

Great dreams are what
makes life worth livin',
n' a lover worth taken
n' a love worth a givin'.

A dreamin' cowboy knows
dreams keep life far from borin'.
They lift up yer spirit
n' friend, they can keep it soarin'!

D.C. Decker   Cowboy Philosopher & Dreamer

LISTEN & LEARN

If you'll get real quiet
many things you could learn.
For all around you
is great knowledge you can earn.

The voice of the Great Spirit
is heard in the twittering birds.
You can learn such mighty things
without saying the words.

You can hear mother nature
tell of her choices.
In the rippling waters
you can hear her wonderous voices.

On this great earth
we see many powers.
In oceans deep,
in beautiful flowers.

When ever we find out
the earth and we are one;
When we know the truth of it
our real day will come.

When we find out
the earth and man are of one mind;
When we know the truth of it
we will all be kind.

D.C. Decker.......   Humble Word Painter

Mother Nature's Water Song!

EAGLE, LION & LAMB

That day I watched an eagle soar.
I felt the spirit of his flight.
O' what a powerful sight to see,
this symbol of freedom and might.

Laid down by a prairie dog village
n' wondered at their plight.
They have family, love and peace,
not war, for they don't fight.

Sand Grouse, wrens n' magpies came,
each had so much to say.
They chirped n' told about
a slight chance of peace today.

Black Crows flew down
not one, but two or three.
They all agreed they used ta' fight
but had enough for all ya' see.

What's the use of fighting
for gain is greater still,
living in peace and harmony
while strugglin' up life's hill.

I sat up on the mound
with my animal friends I'd found.
Things became quite clear to me
as I quietly looked around.

Then came a bunch of rabbits
to greet me safe n' sound.
I shared my food with them
just a sittin' on the ground

I heard some coyotes howl
in the coming silence of the night.
Behold, a lion and a lamb
came bounding into sight.

About time the Eagle winked.
The birds n' animals agreed.
Hatred n' war: there is no need,
no one has the right to greed.

All gathered, we stayed the night
n' watched the campfire burn.
Talked of peace n' man's strange ways
n' wondered if he'd ever learn.

What a fool he's been all his days
Kept blinded by the truth to learn.
Resisted GOD'S knowledge to find
his noble place and not to burn.

D.C. Decker.... Animal Spirit Talker

110

THIS MINUTE IN TIME

My friend, as you ride your range
n' travel life's rocky road.
It's sure important how ya' choose,
I recon you've been told.

So precious is each moment,
it is important, it is prime.
Once it's gone it can't come again,
so understand the value of time.

Time well spent is a blessin' in life
no matter what ya' do
Ridin' broncs or punchin' cows
can be your blessin' too!

It really doesn't matter what ya' do
as long as it is good.
Ya' can do most anythin' ya' choose,
layin' by a river, restin' in the wood.

It don't matter if you're cleanin' stalls
or jus' sleepin' in the hay.
The thing that really matters
is that you're the one ta' plan yer day.

Do some good things for other folks
while yer spendin' time then.
'Cause each minute that passes by
will never come again!

D.C. Decker   **Cowboy Word Painter**

YOUR WORD OL' PARD

I've been ta' the mountain top
n' fell ta' the valleys below.
Yes, I've been in prison
n' I've been in the hole.

My life has been right interestin'
many trails I have rode.
Been full of joys n' heartaches
quite excitin' I've been told.

I loved the wild horses
n' the tame ones too.
Lived several different lives
but the cowboys life is true.

I just want ta' rope n' ride
n' be left alone to do,
the writin' n' lovin'
for the folks that love me too.

Let me ride out where its quiet
n' build a ranch from the start.
Let me do what I need ta' do
'cause it's all right from the heart.

I'll ride n' rope n' write some poems
n' love n' I'll do right.
I can still soar with eagles
ya' can bet I'll try with all my might.

Many things are important in life
but none can hold a candle ta' achieve
the honesty of your word n' truth
n' ta' hold on ta' what ya' believe.

I've made a few mistakes in life,
I guess it could be said of all.
One thing when your word is good
you can ride straight up, settin' tall.

D.C. Decker   **Ol' Cowboy Word Painter**

112

GOLDEN RULE

One to another, love each other.
To love another can be a task.
Give it your all is all one can ask.
Love with your heart but do not smother.
Listen to the words of your precious mother.

Love your neighbor as yourself.
Do unto others as you would have them do unto you!
Make loving and caring the object of your day.
This, your Mighty Maker asks of you.
It is what works, it's tried and true.

If you go through life feeling sad,
If you go through life believing it's bad,
If all the ruckus makes you mad,
If you go through life thinking it's cruel
You undoubtedly don't understand the Golden Rule.

D.C. Decker......... Humble word Painter

THE TRAIL OF LIFE

My ol' hoss n' me
seemed like we'd come to the end of the trail.
Looked like we were lost in spite of our sight
but we'd just come onto a big log rail.

I picked up my reins n' spurred em' to the right
not bein' used to given in to fright.
My ol' hoss n' me went straight on our new way,
made me think a whole lot about life that day.

Sometimes we come to life's crossroads
n' think it is the end.
But the GREAT SPIRIT has a much wider vision,
He knows it is only a bend.

The trail will go on n' get smoother
after you've stopped for a rest.
Your trail that lies hidden beyond
is often the part that is best.

So my friend, stop, relax n' grow stronger,
you n' your ol' hoss take a rest.
Take aim n' worry no longer;
when ridin' keep lookin' up yonder.

HE'LL show you a brighter tomorrow,
without sadness nor sickness nor sorrow.
My friend, let go n' let GOD share your load.
Cause, you've just come to a bend in the road.

D.C. Decker.............Cowboy Trail Rider

I dedicate this poem to all who need to ride on into their great tomorrows, beyond the bend in the trail.   DCD

WHEN GOLDEN DAYS ARE O'ER

When these golden days are o'er
n' I can't ride no more,
I wonder what I'll do then
besides rockin' on the floor.

Don't want to be no spectator
that gives me itchy feet.
I'll get out there and give my best
so I can still compete.

I won't be no spectator
I'll figure somethin' out.
If I just stand around and gawk
I'll surely get the gout.

When these golden days are o'er
n' I can't ride no more,
I'll go ta' the big rodeos
n' tell em' stories galore.

I'll tell em' bout the real west
n' how it was back then.
I'll tell em' how rank n' wild
the stock was a standin' in the pen.

But the big news I will tell em'
is how they came out of the chutes.
They'd jump so high they'd reach the sky
n' bronc riders would shake in their boots.

I recon when we get old n' grey
things get bigger back in the old days.
Your mind goes ta' blowin' things up
n' ya' tend ta' glamorize in many ways.

I recon I'll just stay at the ranch
n' ride Ol' blue.
He's plumb gentle now
n' he's sure tried n' true.

That way I can still be a cowboy
n' with the old timers stand.
I won't have ta' run at the mouth
ta' show em' that I can.

It's alright ta' get older
just keep a movin' ya' see.
Ya' can ride your own home range,
stay healthy, n' that's good enough for me!

D.C. Decker

HERO'S N' LEGENDS

I wanted ta' be a legend in my own time
but I recon it ain't meant to be.
As my life passed through the ages
I was just me ya' see.

Sure I was different they all said,
but many folks come n' go.
A few stand out n' give to others,
these few I want to know.

The west has known many a hero
but fer me n' my hoss Ol' Paint;
we could ride fer ever n' ever
n' brother we just ain't.

I didn't ride with old Custer
n' I'm sure glad of that.
I'm just ridin' Ol' Paint
n' wearin' my cowboy hat.

I wasn't in Buffalo Bill's Wild West Show
or crossed the ocean blue.
I'm just a regular ol' cow puncher
n' damn proud of it too!

I recon I missed a hero's history;
wasn't in the cavalry at the Little Big Horn.
I was meant to be an uncommon man
although it seems no hero or legend born.

I'll ride with uncommon men
in big hats n' boots they go.
They can ride n' rope wild cattle
they ain't just some common Joe.

What we need are more uncommon cowboys
who are legends in their own mind.
Folks love cowboy hero's n' legends
'cause they are of the good ol' kind...................

D.C. Decker...............   Cowboy Philosopher

FINALLY, I SAY FINALLY

I die each day
I die each day now.

I have been strong in life and love,
leaned into the mighty winds of life.
Rode the wild buckin' horses.
Have taken on missions, lived in fine abodes
n' traveled down some lonesome roads.

I've shown more courage than most,
often succeeded, often failed.
All in all I cannot boast.
Have provided much for many, disappointed a few
as I have been disappointed too!

I have loved fully, my precious children number five.
We all thank God they are well and alive.
I love them very much, wouldn't you.
We love each other sure it's true,
I also love their mothers too!

I have owned land as far as the eye could see;
great horses and the cattle on seven hills in quantity.
I've lived a life of honesty,
many times been misunderstood.
But of course I knew they would.

I've felt betrayed, withdrew into myself,
slowly died and said ado.
I have dreamed dreams and made them come true,
crossed the oceans to help a few.
Looked on all others as brothers too!

I have been there to see the sickle and the wall fall.
Went to the Holy Mountain Carmel to give my all.
Been misunderstood? Even hated by a few.
They knew me not you can bet 'tis true.
For my creed is, "I will give to you."

I have never hated, extending love and support,
wanting to be understood in the knowledge I report.
I have always loved them, then we'd drift apart,
in the process of tearing up my heart.
Know full well I have lived life right from the start.

I die each day now, I die each day,
for they have finally wounded me.
I die each day, the world has found a way.
Finally, my wounded heart grieves
for it is broken and I am on my knees.

I hear a voice from up above, "WAIT, you cannot die.
It is I who made you, so you can stand the strife.
Get up, fly like a loving dove, I will give you life!
I have sent you love once more, all your friends remain.
Get back to the D.C. Decker spirit, then you will sustain."

Dear God, I'll saddle up my best horse, ride with style n' grace.
I can ride into the wind again, there's nothing I can't face.
I can embrace a common place n' soar with eagles on a chase.
I'll create, n' love n' give my all.
You can bet your life I'll be ridin' tall!

D.C.Decker.......... Humble Word Painter

119

RODEO DAYS

D. C. DECKER

RODEO DAYS

THESE ARE POEMS MOSTLY
ABOUT MY YOUNGER DAYS ON
WILD WEST SHOWS AND THEN
CONTEST RODEOS. I GUESS IT
WAS DIFFERENT THEN. IT WAS A
TOUGH OL' ROAD WITH MANY
FRIENDS TO HELP ALONG THE
WAY. I REMEMBER MOST ALL OF
THEM JUST LIKE IT WERE
YESTERDAY. I GUESS IT WAS. I
KNOW, TODAY IT TAKES THE
SAME SPIRIT IT DID BACK IN THE
DAYS OF CASEY, DEB, HARRY
AND JIM. I WAS NEVER IN THEIR
CLASS BUT THEY WERE FRIENDS
AND SO WERE MANY MORE.
MANY HAVE GONE ON TO THE BIG
PASTURE UP ON HIGH. I MISS EM'
STILL.

RODEO

The Rodeo meant so much to me
when I was growin' up back then.
It still does today, when I see a buckin' chute
or broncs standin' in a pen.

It's done on many levels
'cause we ain't all world champs.
It goes from the National Finals
clear down ta' the ol' cow camps.

We all think we're great bronc riders
n' ropers n' can work all events.
But most of us ain't quite that good
n' have ta' stay at the ranch n' mend the fence.

We admire the great champions
n' love ta' watch em' ride.
We can even ride them bulls
in the livin' room on the old cowhide.

Now I've been ta' the big ones
n' drawed up real good.
Nearly got bucked off in the chute
like ol' Jake said I would.

I recon I ain't no champ
still I love that rodeo.
Don't matter how big or small
ta' the rodeo I want ta' go.

I'm goin' ta' try them saddle broncs
once more before I die.
I probably won't win no championship
but ya' can bet yer ranch I'll try.

I'll draw them good high kickin' broncs
n' start em' out just right.
I'll ride em' with ol' Casey's style
n' ride em' keen with all my might.

123

BROTHER TOM

BROTHER TOM

Ol' Pard let me tell ya'
just how it's always been.
I've got a favorite partner
he just happens to be kin.

We've rode some range together
n' most times we rode apart.
But no matter how distant the range
he's always in my heart.

I've always admired my brother Tom
even though he's younger than me.
When we were kids he could ride a horse
n' beat me up a tree.

We went rodeoin' at an early age.
There was John, the Button, Tom n' me.
Pretty good hands I'd gage.
Bareback ridin' was Tom's specialty.

Tom was a fine champion many times.
He could ride n' spur em' with the best.
He won the All-Around one year
winnin' many a tough contest.

But all that was just a part of Tom,
many talents he possessed.
He has a big fine family
he's taken care of with his natural zest.

Pardner I love him n' admire all he's done.
He's wise n' smart, knows lots of things.
He loves the west n' cowboy art, n' as for me
I THINK HE SOARS ON EAGLES WINGS!

D.C. Decker

RODEO

ENJOY YOURSELF IN A WESTERN WAY

· DECKER RODEO · PRODUCTION · OFFICIAL · PROGRAM 25¢ · 100 YEARS · OF PROGRESS ·

Decker's 4D Ranch

THE BUTTON & THE BULL

The Button climbed up on the chute gate
with his bull rope in his hand.
He could hear the cheerin' of the crowds
and the playin' of the band.

But his thoughts were on his sweetheart
and the time they'd have that night
for he was settin' high up in the average
n' first money was in sight.

D.C. Decker - Rodeo Clown   7/4/58

He placed his rope down on the bull
not up too far or back.
He gentle eased down on em'
while his partner pulled the slack.

With his hand tensed in the bullrope
n' his spurs in Tornado's hide
he didn't yell or hollar
he just quietly said, "outside".

Now ol' Tornado was a twistin' spinner
the kind that's seldom rode.
How the Button stayed 8 seconds
that stories often told.

But with a final plunging leap
the Button hit the ground.
The bull ignored the flashing cap
of the nimble footed clown.

When the dust had settled
n' the bull was drawn away.
I could see at a glance
that the kid was down ta' stay.

His life was growing dim
his breath was fading fast.
He told me to tell his sweetheart
that bull was to have been his last.

When the rodeo was over
we were all feelin' down.
N' I had to tell his sweetheart,
'cause I was that rodeo clown.

D.C. Decker   Rodeo Word Painter

MIGHTY SLIM PICKENS

In all the annuals of rodeo clowns
there were many great ones ya' see
n' one of the best was
Ol' Slim Pickens if you're askin' me.

In his time he was the best
at rodeo comedy
n' he could fight them bulls
in that Mexican style ya' see.

He'd wear his funny "Trage De Luces"
n' unfold his big ol' cape.
He was ready ta' fight the bulls
n' help keep the riders in good shape.

Slim Pickens was a great character
n' a good actor too.
He could be a fine cowhand one day
n' the next do what actors do.

He was a fine storyteller
n' he could make ya' laugh a lot.
Ol' Slim had lots of friends,
he was a good man n' deep within.

He lived a full n' entertainin' life
n' he gave the world a fine hand.
He was a legend in his time
n' ta' me he was just grand.

I fought a few bulls in my own "Trage"
n' fought em' with my cape out west.
But friend, I got ta' tell ya'
Ol' Slim Pickens was the best!

D.C. Decker....   _Old Rodeo Clown_
                         Bull Fighter
                         Cowboy Word Painter

SPOTTED EAGLE

It was back about 1963
my days on the saddle broncs.
I drew ol' Spotted Eagle,
at buckin' cowboys off he was mighty good.
I'd sure try ta' ride em' if I could.

He was kind of a purdy horse
n' he was sure nuff solid.
He was always fat n' slick
n' there's more ta' mention.
He'd buck so hard he'd get yer attention.

Ol' Spotted Eagle would bog his head,
then he'd duck n' dive n' throw it in the air.
This horse could buck n' kick
n' if ya' could ride em' fair
ya' could win a big ridin' most anywhere.

So when he cleared the chutes
n' bog his head way down.
I just turn my toes out
n' spurred em' like ya' should.
Then I went n' rode em' like I knew I could.

I won a ridin' on Spotted Eagle
n' I was sure happy that day.
I could ride a fair buckin' horse,
sometimes when well, sometimes in pain
I could ride em' cause Casey made my rein!

DC Decker

HOME RANCH RODEO ARENA

THE FARMER SADDLE BRONC

There was this big brown buckin' horse
big hooves n' a big ol' head of course.
Had a long black flowin' mane
The Farmer was his name.

When cowboys drawed him they'd get the jitters.
He stood 17 hands at the whithers.
Could barely fit into the buckin' chutes,
caused many a hand ta' shake in their boots.

He could jump n' kick n' duck n' dive,
a great buckin' horse with a lot of size.
Many a year he rodeoed,
no one rode em', they all got throwed.

Ol' Morgan owned him with stock contractors pride
I sure wanted ta' draw em', I knew I could ride.
My wish was granted, but he bucked me off so high
I thought I was given solo rights ta' fly.

I lasted just five seconds, the flyin' was alright,
but when I hit the ground it shook me up a mite!
As I hobbled back to the buckin' chutes
Ol' Morgan was a laughin' in his boots.

Yep, the Farmer had his way that day
but ol' Morgan had better pray,
'cause the next time I draw em'
I'll ride em' n' surely have my way.

The next time came late that fall
n' I didn't last no time at all.
Ol' Farmer flipped in the chute
n' squashed me hard ta' boot.

Then winter came n' rodeos went indoors,
in fancy places with heat n' floors.
I entered saddle broncs n' bulls, I was in awe
to know how lucky I was in the draw.

Well hell, how lucky can I be,
I drawed up mighty good for me.
The bull was YoYo, he's never been rode.
Yep, the bronc was Farmer, all got throwed!

The time had come for me ta' show
if I could win at the big rodeo.
The horse had won two times before
I was goin' ta' win this ridin' war.

Put my saddle on em' gently boy.
Let's keep em' quiet he's not a toy.
I need a clean jump out of the chute
n' Dear GOD be with me ta' boot!

My turn had come, I measured my rein,
wanted ta' get out before he flipped again.
I nodded my head, I must be insane,
Farmer cleared the gate like a hurricane.

He done his thing that big ol' horse.
He jumped n' kicked n' bucked his best of course.
I rode em' right fancy n' spurred em' every lick.
The crowd liked my ride, they knew I was no hick.

Finally, the whistle blew,
I said, "Ol' Farmer I've conquered you!"
I respected that big ol' horse,
when he was a buckin' he was a mighty force.

As history shows for many a year,
when ol' Farmer was great n' most severe
I was the only one ta' ride em' clean
n' go ta' the pay window, ya' know what I mean.

DC Decker........ Word Paintin' Bronc Rider

SAD RODEO CLOWN

Have you ever seen a sad rodeo clown
with tears running down?
His makeup starting to smear
as he tries to hold back the tear.

Bull riding was the next event,
he hoped they'd fight, he had to vent.
His heart was heavy, the pain was great,
his precious mother had met her fate.

He wiped away the painful tear
in losing one he held so dear.
The bulls were rank, the riders fell
the bulls were fast, they fought like hell.

The next one out was a spinnin' bull,
the rider bucked down in the hole.
The clown jumped in to save his life
that was his duty n' role.

The clown fought the bulls recklessly
tryin' to get rid of the pain.
He fought em' with wild abandon,
no fear in spite of the strain.

The crowd stood up cheering
they knew not the cause.
The whole rodeo was shaken
from the wild applause.

The last one was to be rode,
a wild fightin' bull I was told.
I got down on hands n' knee
n' made that ol' bull come to me.

PAINTING THE MASK—Donnie Decker, featured clown with the Mid-Western Horse Show and Rodeo, dons his grease paint for Monday's matinee at the Ohio State Fairgrounds. He went on with two shows after learning Sunday that his mother had died in Toledo of brain cancer.

Mom Dies, but Clowns Go on With the Show

By JACKSON S. ELLIOTT

The bull was mad, I was glad
but oh so sad.
We fought it out alright
until we both ran out of fight.

Then the silence came, I had to go,
it was the pain, I guess you'd know.
Dearest mother needed me
to put her in the ground so low.

The Rodeo Committee paid me well
said, "God bless, and farewell".
We all know you will excel
and live many years to tell.

I took the grease paint off my face
n' headed home, no time to waste.
I just knew she'd found a better home
I'd just weep awhile, then write this poem.

D.C. Decker......Sad Rodeo Clown

GOIN' DOWN THE ROAD

In the early days of travelin'
to the rodeo.
It didn't matter whether contest
or just a wild west show.

It was hard on all of us
goin' down some bumpy road
in old junk cars
n' movin' slower than a toad.

With red n' bread
the meal of the day
n' money bein' scarce
n' not findin' our way.

Some how a miracle
would get us there.
Like we were rough n' wild
but still in His care.

We'd pull into the rodeo grounds
pool our money ta' enter.
Hope we'd draw up good
n' ride ta' come out a winner.

Sometimes gettin' one horse rode
ken sure mean a lot ta' a fella.
Specially if he's far from home
n' has spent his last dolla.

Not countin' bein' hungry
'cause that was the case a lot.
But bein' boogered up n' hurtin'
might keep em' from the top.

When we would draw a good un'
our buddies would pull the slack.
They'd measure off yer buck rein
n' tell ya', "spur em' in the neck."

Once in awhile we'd get lucky
n' one of us would win.
We'd a least have enough money
so we could go again.

The road got mighty bumpy
goin' ta' the next big rodeo.
But we just kept agoin' down the road
a havin' fun ya' know

D.C. Decker

THE WHISTLE

In all my days of rodeoin'
I've heard many a good sound.
It was the clankin' of buckin' chutes
n' the jokes of the funny clown.

You sometimes hear
the cheerin' of the crowd
or the playin' of the band,
or cowboys a yellin' loud.

The rodeo has a lot of sounds
distinct in the cowboys world.
From the bulls a bellerin'
ta' the many stories told.

But the greatest sound I ever heard
was while ridin' for my honey.
Just ta' hear that whistle blow
n' thinkin' I'd won some money.

D.C.Decker.........   Cowboy Word Painter.

BOOGER RED

I once knew this cowboy
his name was Booger Red.
He was a wild bronc rider,
now ol' Booger Red is dead.

He went ta' this big ol' rodeo
way back before buckin' chutes.
They'd snub them wild ones
n' cowboys were shaken in their boots.

Bronc Busters would crawl on em'
over the backs of the snubbin' hoss.
Once they got their stirrups
they'd nod down at the boss.

The boss would yell,"turn em' loose."
n' off the bucker would go.
The broncs were wild n' they could buck
they'd snort n' sunfish n' blow.

Well, ol' Booger drawed ol' Midnight
the rankest in the herd.
When booger went up ta' the snubbin' hoss
nary a sound was heard.

He got down on ol' Midnight
n' listened for the bosses call.
Midnight rared up n' jerked em' down,
Booger Red, the snubbin' hoss n' all.

With all the scamblin' on the ground,
Booger Red got kicked in the head.
Everybody prayed for him,
but Booger Red was dead.

D.C. Decker...   Sad Cowboy Word Painter

WILD WEST SHOW

Back in the days of the wild west show
we'd travel from town to town.
Puttin' on the best in the west.
For that we were renown.

I loved the old wild west show.
Good characters hung around.
They were rich in story tellin'
'bout the country n' bout the town.

Each seemed ta' have a specialty,
the trick riders ride, the ropers threw.
Was some of the best in all the world
n' I got ta' know em' too!

There was Rex Rossi n' Jackie Rhinehart,
Jim Eskew, George Taylor,
n' Patty Aton n' many more.
Yes, I could go on and on.

There was ol' Fog Horn Clancy
always on the mike.
Tellin' all the folks that came,
the grown-ups and the tykes.

He told what was goin' on
in his own special style.
He helped em' understand the show
he joked and made em' smile.

The clowns were really funny then
like ol' George Mills n' Wilber Plaugher,
Toad n' Licille Harris n' so many more.
More than I can name.

I watched the roughstock riders
some of em' down on their luck.
I could tell they could do it once
as I watched the livestock buck.

I loved the smell, the whole damned place,
you see I was just a kid.
But eventually in the rush of time
I did it all, I did!

D.C. Decker

ENTRY FEES

Way back in early times
a rodeoin' we did go.
I was damned near broke
if ya' really need ta' know.

We'd spent our last dollar
for red n' bread n' gas.
The truth now known
we were broke on our ass.

Our old car gave out
at the rodeo gate.
I had ta' borrow money
n' this I hate.

Here comes our buddy.
"Hey John could ya' enter me?"
We sat down fer a minute
under a big ol' shade tree.

I'll give ya' a quarter
of my winnin's friend
or I could pay ya' back
when I get on the mend.

I know I'll draw up good
at this here rodeo.
I'll start em' right
n' spur em' hard ya' know.

Without much hesitation
ol' John smiled at me.
He reached in his Levi pocket
n' handed me a wrinkled twenty.

Now this day I was lucky
n' won the saddle bronc day money.
I was able ta' pay ol' John
n' some left over for my honey.

Some days when I had a bankroll
I'd enter up a hand.
We all try ta' help each other
in any way we can.

DCD

141

CODY WILD WEST SHOW

William F. Cody was a real hero
in many important ways.
It's not about the wars he fought
no, it's about the wild west days.

He did so many things
they are hard to imagine.
He was bigger than life
n' he is a true legend.

A bold frontiersman he was
n' a showman of great fame.
He was a pretty good businessman
William F. Cody was his name.

He was born on the Iowa prairie
in the year of 1846.
The exciting story of his life
is really hard ta' fix.

Ol' Russell & Company took em' in at ten
a workin' on the wagon trains.
He worked big cattle drives
n' rode across the plains.

In 1860 he rode for the pony express
n' started his notoriety.
He rode the fastest 322 miles one time
n' became famous in western society.

But he was still a kid back then
his feats had just begun.
When barely 22 he gets a big job
gettin' meat for the railroad with his gun.

Ol' William F. Cody made history
n' he got a new name.
Killin' buffalo for the railroad
for two years was his game.

In that short career it is noted
he killed over 4000 head.
From then on he was **Buffalo Bill**
n' became famous throughout the land.

The Buffalo Bill Wild West Show
was the biggest n' best in the world
that gigantic story
is yet to be properly told.

D.C. Decker   Cowboy Word Painter

HORSES I'VE KNOWN

ABOUT THE ONLY REAL
ADDICTION I HAVE HAD IN MY
LIFE WOULD BE HORSES. THEY
HAVE AFFORDED ME MUCH. I
BECAME A HORSE WHISPERER
AT THE AGE OF 8. MORE
IMPORTANTLY BY THE TIME I
WAS 12 I WAS A HORSE
LISTENER. I LEARNED A LOT
FROM THEM. MOST OF MY
FRIENDS WERE PUTTING IT ON
HORSES THE HARD WAY. I
NEVER UNDERSTOOD THAT. I
ALWAYS FELT MOST OF EM'
WOULD LIKE TO BE TREATED IN
A FRIENDLY MANNER. I'VE
OWNED SOME DAMNED SURE
GOOD ONES AND A FEW OF THE
OTHER KIND. IN ALL THEY'D BE
TO NUMEROUS TO MENTION SO
I'LL JUST GIVE YA' A FEW.

COWBOY SOFT SPOT

This ol' cowboy named D.C. Decker
ranched in the Osage west of Tulsee Town.
His life reflects a timeliness of old
n' a truth of some renown.

Out where the prairies roll n' mountains rise,
where cowpokes work n' play.
Ol' D.C. sees the wonderment in every tree.
He holds ta' the moments in the passing of a day.

Sees life where some would say, there aint' none,
don't like it we've lost the big open range
He looks around n' knows his love still lives there.
He's a cowboy n' don't cater much to change.

In time his old west may fade away,
but he'll still find the wonder where,
that big bronc bustin' n' cattle scene
stands plumb vivid over there.

He still sees romance in the setting sun,
when it shoots long shadows thru night leaved trees.
He loves horses n' ugly pokes,
with wrinkled hands, n' wisdom n' squinty eyes he sees.

His eyes have seen many shiny trails,
a few cities in the haze.
He loves the west where special kinds of people live,
in lovin', friendly, workin' ways.

This home growed cowboy n' horseman,
we've come to realize,
has this great big soft spot
for all the horses he sees through his western eyes.

When standin' by his cabin or by the old barn door,
they come right up to him 'cause they know he's kind.
He sees their beauty, grace n' strength,
he sure is soft on em' you'll find.

Ol, D.C. talks to them n' then he listens too!
If you ever wonder 'bout this ol' horseman, n' many often do,
he's got this big ole soft spot for the horse.
And he's got it thru n' thru!

D.C. Decker

FISTFULL
1958 Reining Champion

OL' PAINT

I've owned a lot of horses
in my time.
Some were mighty good ones
n' some wher'nt worth a dime.

One day I stood a leanin'
against the old barn door.
Ol' Paint he wanted in
on the barn's old wooden floor.

Now he was one of the best ones
a man could ever own.
But he could buck a lick
n' many times I got thrown.

Once you got him topped for the day
a better cow horse you couldn't find.
He was fast n' had a lot of cow
but ya' couldn't read his mind.

One day he wanted to be a bronc
n' the next day be was gentle n' kind.
Workin' a cow he was quick as a cat but
like I tell ya, ya couldn't read his mind.

Here he is a nudgin' me jus' ta let him in,
could it be the old oat bin is callin' him?
It's not feedin' time, he knows that
when I stumbled a mite n' kicked the cat.

Ol' Paint saw an openin' n' ran in soon,
headed right straight for the saddle room.
He ran in an stood by his own saddle with pride,
all Ol' Paint wanted was to go for a ride.

D.C. Decker   Horse Whisperer
                               Word Painter

148

THE HORSE WHISPERER

Some feller named Nicholas Evans recently wrote a book.
He told in a pretty good way about a horse whisperer
from up Montana way named Tom Booker.
He wrote a real fine story n' I sure know it's true
'cause I've been one since I was 4ft. 2.

In my day there was horse breakers n' bronc peelers too.
Many an outlaw could shake a man up n' then try to eat you.
The horses were rank n' wild n' free,
they were as ornery as can be,
n' ridin' em' was mighty tough, now can't you see.

Most of the hands were tougher than hell,
used quirts, n' spurs, hit em' hard n' made em' swell.
It worked for some but I recon I had a better way
to train em' up n' have them work for you each day.
I'd just whisper to em', that's how I got my say.

I rode into this big outfit many years ago.
They were tryin' to get their hosses broke, if you'd like to know.
All the hands were getting' throwed down hard,
the scene was wild n' wooly I'm tellin' ya' pard,
n' to make it worse the women were all laughin' standin' in the yard.

I recon a feller might truly say
these boys were havin' a real tough day.
I rode on up n' looked em' over, 20 head I saw.
An ornery bunch alright, rough for the average hand to draw.
At this point the horses were winning about 20 to naw.

Sir, I see your horse herd ain't getting' very tame.
I can get em' trained for you 'cause hosses are my game.
Send your boys back to' punchin' cows before they are all lame.
The old man looked at me'
kid these are big rank horses can't you see?

You're too small n' you're still wet behind the ears.
La me tell ya' sir, I may not have the years,
but I can train em' to stop n' turn n' how to gage them steers.
Get those waddies out of here n' I'll show ya' what I mean.
I'm the best horse whisperer that you have ever seen.

Hell son, I'll give ya' a try, what do I have to loose?
Let me tell ya' ol' man, if you so choose,
it'll cost ya' 20 silver dollars n' 20 sacks of oats
n' it'll cost ya' more than that add 20 head of goats.
N' besides I want it quiet round here 'cause that's what counts the most.

Now I don't want no teachin', got my own way if you don't mind.
Recon I'll run em' in the round pen so we can spend some time,
just a whisperin' n' talkin' n' treatin' em right kind.
The ol' rancher looked at me, he didn't understand,
but he said, "it's yer job little man, I'd like to watch you if I can."

Ya' all can watch I don't mind, jus' want it plumb quiet for a time.
Herd ran into the round pen n' I leaned against the snubbin' post.
Recon I stood there for hours, studyin' the rank ones most.
I pointed out this big black outlaw,
n' tells the ol' boss, he'll be ready for your mother in law.

In just a few days ya' can bet they'll all ride good a follerin' my ways.
I never took a whip to em, jus' talked straight n' put rope halters on.
They ran in circles with their lead ropes draggin' on the ground.
For awhile they'd hear me but sill go round n' round.
In awhile they'd stop n' listen to my ever sound.

Horses are a lot like people, in their feelin's n' actions too.
Trainin' em to' do what ya' want comes from how you do.
If ya' talk to em' n' whisper what ya' want n' tell em' true
ya' can bet yer boots they'll follow you
n' give their hearts, n' go to work n' stick like glue.

So if you want to be a hoss trainer
the first thing you must do
is get ta' know em' real good
n' let em' know the Golden Rule.
Treat em' kind even if it's a mule.

Be a good horse whisperer
then they can understand
just who you are n' what
you want, then you'll find
they really can!

D.C. Decker

Horse Whisperer
Word Painter

OTHER POEMS

I LIKE TO WRITE ABOUT MY
OTHER FRIENDS, THE INDIANS
AND OTHER FOLKS WHO ARE
GREAT BUT NOT COWBOYS.
HERE'S A FEW.

154

I TOO CARE

I am a Raven Warrior chosen to defend my people.
I have the heart of softness within a warrior's stone.
I fight to keep our freedom we all are brothers,
we are brothers all. I will ride tall. We should all
have rights equal upon this earth. No man born
free can be contented when penned up and denied
his liberty.

We all were made by the Great Creator to go
where we choose to go. Mother Earth is for all of
us, even this the white man should know. I am
but an Indian but I too care about man's freedom
for all of those who dare. If man could know the
truth of things their spirits would rise and they
would become good friends right before your eyes.

DC Decker...   Friend of the Indian

TEPEE TRUTH

In the tepee or round the campfire
only truth was told.
Truth was the strength of the people
in the days of old.
Real truth's still best for all
O' people please hear its call.
Should not allow in any acts
false beliefs to take the place of facts.
False beliefs condemn mentality
for truth is our sacred reality.
It gives us all the real power
to see GOD'S LIGHT every hour.
Seek the truth with all your might
what ever you do it will be right.
What ever it is you wish to achieve
it will be granted to those who believe.
No matter what color you are my friend
we are all GOD'S children in the end.
Seek the truth with all your heart
it'll bring you freedom from the start.
Truth, the essence of wisdom n' knowledge
keeps us safe from the world of folly.

D.C. Decker   Cowboy Philosopher
                               Word Painter

156

LIFE'S A JOURNEY

Cowboys n' cowgirls know this for a fact
you're supposed to have fun, you're not comin' back.
Life is to be lived, there is much to learn.
It's just part of a trip if you're concerned.

Life is not a destination, no sirree
it's a wonderful journey can't you see.
It's full of bumps and curves tis' true,
has turning points n' mountains n' valleys too!

Everything that comes our way
shapes n' molds us each n' everyday.
In this great adventure with all its strife
we discover the best in ourselves; n' that's life!

D.C. Decker   Cowboy Philosopher

GOOD GOAL

O' Great Spirit
Our goals are but to follow
in ways that lead to You!
There is no higher goal
that this you see.
What could we need but Thee?

When in our hearts we seek
to find our identity,
We discover it cannot be done
until we come to Thee!
Your Spirit gave us life,
Without You we make it a tragedy.

d.c.d.   5/1/96

BE YOURSELF

Forgive yourself in all you do.
Forgive all the others too!
Forget the slander you have heard.
Forget the hasty unkind word.

Forget the quarrel and the cause.
Forget the whole affair because
Forgiving is the only way.
Forget the storms of yesterday.

Forget the one whose sour face
Forgets to smile in any place.
Be yourself and give off kindness
Even if the world is still in blindness.........

d.c.d.   5/15/96

WHITE MAN - INDIAN MAN

For many many moons now
I've walked a lonely walk
I wanted to see how
Always hoping, sometimes in fright
Coming near neither could see me
I pray and talk of peace
Still they fight.
We talk but no response is heard.
We hold stupid prejudice
Not even the kindness of a word
Not long ago in all the silence
I burned the sage to clean the air
So they will come and set in peace
So they will come to show they care
Their hearts tell lies
They are not sincere
So any unity dies

Not long ago I smoked my pipe of peace
I smoke it alone
No one to pass it to
Alone in silence I get down
Alone in silence I get blue
Then I pass the great words of peace
I write the words, I say the words
No one hears, no one cares
No one listens, not even the birds
It takes peace and unity
To mend the sacred circle
To bring harmony and peace
To the whole community
In my lonely place
I am a caring one
I feel alone
I am
I

D.C. Kicking Horse   Spirit Painter

SIOUX PRAYER

I hope the Great Heavenly Father, who will look down upon us, will give all the tribes His Blessing, that we may go forth in peace, and live in peace all our days, and that He will look down upon our children and finally lift us far above this earth; and that our Heavenly Father will look upon our children as His children, that all the tribes may be His children, and as we shake hands we may forever live in peace.

Hear the voice of Red Cloud, Marpiya Luta, Oglala Sioux.

GONE YET HERE

Every semblance, every shape
that perisheth today,
in the treasure house of time
is safely stored away.
When the earth,
revolves to it's higher place
out of the invisible He draweth
forth it's face.

The duty of long years of love obey,
to tell the tale of happy days gone by.
Land and sky may laugh aloud today,
gladden mind and heart
and just won't die...

They are gone, I caused it so.
My heart is grieved, now you know.
I will tell some other day,
this parting hurt and woe.
Let us write some other way,
Love's secrets; better so!
Leave blood and noise and heart's desire'
then peace can come again to grow!

D.C. Decker

It's your dream.
Your sweat.
Your time, your investment.
You win some. You lose some.
But you keep trying.
Because you're committed to your ideal.
And ultimately, to your decision.
You don't take such things lightly.

About this author, it's hard to say. He's lived many lifetimes and lifestyles in less than six and one half decades. He has lived life to the fullest. With all of its ups and downs, he remains a very spiritual person, full of thankfulness for the great wonderment of life. D.C. Decker has owned many ranches, raising fine cattle and horses. He tells us he loves animals and people but he doesn't know which he loves best. We'd guess it would be animals.

Quiet friend.......

It's your dream.
Your sweat.
Your time, your investment.
You win some. You lose some.
But you keep trying.
Because you're committed to your ideal.
And ultimately, to your decision.

You don't take such things lightly.

About this author, it's hard to say. He's lived many lifetimes and lifestyles in less than six and one half decades. He has lived life to the fullest. With all of its ups and downs, he remains a very spiritual person, full of thankfulness for the great wonderment of life. D.C. Decker has owned many ranches, raising fine cattle and horses. He tells us he loves animals and people but he doesn't know which he loves best. We'd guess it would be animals.

Quiet friend.......

1999 The Year of the Cowboy

NATIONAL COWBOY HALL OF FAME AND WESTERN HERITAGE CENTER

www.ingramcontent.com/pod-product-compliance
Lightning Source LLC
Chambersburg PA
CBHW081229090426

42738CB00016B/3233